logolounge | MASTERlibrary

3000 ANIMAL & MYTHOLOGY LOGOS

DO NOT REMOVE | PROPERTY OF:

DATE RECEIVED:	RECEIVED FROM:

CONTRIBUTOR'S NAME:

BILL GARDNER

ANDREAS KARL

TRACY SABIN

MICHAEL VANDERBYL

volume 2

logolounge | **MASTER** library

3000 ANIMAL & MYTHOLOGY LOGOS
FROM LOGOLOUNGE.COM

BEVERLY MASSACHUSETTS

ROCKPORT PUBLISHERS

catharine fishel and bill gardner

First published in the United States of America by
Rockport Publishers, a member of
Quayside Publishing Group
100 Cummings Center
Suite 406-L
Beverly, Massachusetts 01915-6101
Telephone: (978) 282-9590
Fax: (978) 283-2742
www.rockpub.com

Library of Congress Cataloging-in-Publication Data
Gardner, Bill.
   LogoLounge, master library. Volume 2 : 3000 animal & mythology logos / Bill Gardner and Catharine Fishel.
       p. cm. — (LogoLounge, master library ; v. 2)
   Includes index.
   ISBN-13: 978-1-59253-612-2
   ISBN-10: 1-59253-612-3
   1. Logos (Symbols)—Catalogs. 2. Corporate image—Catalogs. I. Fishel, Catharine M. II. Title. III. Title: 3000 animal & mythology logos. IV. Title: Three thousand animal and mythology logos.
   NC1002.L63F59 2010b
   741.6—dc22
                                                                        2010001784

ISBN-13: 978-1-59253-612-2
ISBN-10: 1-59253-612-3

10 9 8 7 6 5 4 3 2 1

Design: Gardner Design
Layout & Production: *tabula rasa* graphic design
Production Coordinator: Lauren Kaiser / Gardner Design
Cover Image: Gardner Design

Printed in China

To Saul and Paul.

—*Bill Gardner*

Thank you to all of the ever-generous designers who are so willing to inspire others; to Bill and the LogoLounge team for this ongoing opportunity; to my three amazing sons, two majoring in graphic design and the youngest of whom is showing every sign of falling into the brink; and to my best friend and husband, Denny, for being the most thoughtful person on earth.

—*Catharine Fishel*

LogoLounge.com is the world's largest database of logo designs where, in real-time, members can post their logo design work; study the work of others; search a database of more than 130,000 logo designs by keyword, designer's name, client, industry, and other attributes; learn from articles and news written expressly for and about logo designers; build lightboxes for inspiration; and much more. Anyone visiting the site has access to editorial materials, although only members have access to search, upload, and lightbox functions.

LogoLounge is also parent to two lines of bestselling books about logo design, published by Rockport Publishers:

- The original LogoLounge series (1, 2, 3, 4, and 5; Book 6 is under development now)

- The Master Library series, built from seven volumes, each of which contains 3,000 topic-specific logos. The topics covered will be Initials & Crests; Animals & Mythology; Typography; People; Shapes & Symbols; Nature & Food; and Arts & Culture.

For more details, please visit www.LogoLounge.com.

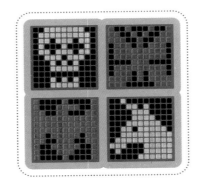

contents

FROM THE
LOGOLOUNGE.COM
INTERNATIONAL
COLLECTION

Expanded
Collections of
LogoLounge
Identity
Categories

introduction

❧ A symbol of fertility, quickness, vulnerability, softness, and more, the rabbit—like many animals—holds many different significant meanings as a potential logo candidate.

⁖ Consider the rabbit—or, for purposes of this discussion, the bunny. The Easter Bunny, although it is a mythical creature (born of Christian culture), is clearly based on a real animal from the real world. It's soft, cute, cuddly, and on a symbolic level, representative of fertility.

It is based on a real animal that, over time, has been imbued with human characteristics. It (somehow) brings gifts of candy and eggs, is often portrayed wearing clothing, can be shown walking upright and smiling, and is, in general, regarded as a benevolent creature that likes to please children, like a favorite uncle.

People who have historically had the Easter Bunny as part of their culture buy into all of this 100 percent, even the implausible parts. At some level, they believe in the Easter Bunny.

Now consider another bunny, the Playboy bunny, who turns the entire rabbit equation on its—well, ears. This icon is represented in two ways: by the company's logo and by young women dressed up as the animal. Ironically, these human versions have been symbolically successful because they adopt the exact same positive attributes as the more wholesome Easter Bunny: soft, cute, cuddly, and representative—in a very different way—of fertility. (Imagine how immensely unsuccessful either would be if they picked up on negative attributes of rabbits, such as leaving droppings everywhere and having large, yellow, sharp incisors.)

People believe that the Easter Bunny and the Playboy bunny (the logo or the fishnet-stockinged version) are "real" because we believe that rabbits are real. Our understanding of or belief in the physical and conceptual attributes of any creature—its "realness"—is a powerful tool, often developed in childhood and reinforced over many years' worth of parables and experience. It becomes part of our toolkit for forming opinions and making decisions.

Belief forms the bridge between real and imagined. It is what allows our brains to easily accept that a rabbit can somehow get into our house to deliver jelly beans (which aren't really beans, but that's a whole different story), or that a simple logo can somehow represent a bricks-and-mortar company.

ANIMALS

The power that animals have over humans is amazing. From the moment children are born, their parents surround them with stuffed animals, images of animals on clothing and décor, and books about animals. Adults teach children lessons and morals using stories about animals. Children come to understand the world through animal analogies and metaphor—"stubborn as a mule" or "clever as a fox."

In this way, people grow to understand the real and sometimes unfairly inflicted personalities of animals. They know which are "good" and which are "bad." For instance, a skunk may be strikingly colored and have very soft fur, but it has one single attribute that lands it with a thud in the "bad" category. A dog, on the other hand, might also smell awful as well as bite and ruin the carpet, but it is almost universally categorized as "good." Dogs are loyal; skunks stink.

Animals are so powerful as symbols that people will apply their image in the form of a tattoo to the skin, graphically adopting the conceptual nature of that animal. Images of animals are used as sports mascots the world round that people stay fiercely loyal to all of their lives.

Designers can use this preexisting knowledge and belief in their logo design. If an owl is understood to be wise, then a logo that includes an owl might suggest wisdom on the part of the company it represents. It's a boost toward understanding.

Animals that really exist in our world (as well as extinct ones) offer special advantages for the logo designer. Some have a unique and easily traded-upon shape. For instance, the outline of a giraffe is very simple to identify, whereas that of a weasel may be confused with a ferret or otter. Even the outline of a snake or other "scary" animal is safer to the brain than that of an unidentifiable monster. The more familiar the shape, the more information it conveys.

A unique shape, especially if it is very simple—such as a butterfly—is graphically impactful and easy to remember. Also, humans have a certain compassion for animals and might feel more emotionally connected to an animal-shaped logo than they would to a hard-edged, geometric design. Animals are simply more like us.

Some animals carry multiple messages. For instance, birds can be a symbol of peace, flight, launch, song, nesting, and much more. Just using their wings makes a statement, even when they are applied to objects as unlikely as a coffee cup or the letter H.

An animal can also be used to suggest a region or topography: A loon might suggest a North American fishing camp or a horse can suggest a Western ranch. Animals are also often used to indicate nationalism, as a kangaroo represents Australia, and an eagle represents the United States. Or, an animal can represent a more figurative arena, as doves often are used to represent Christianity.

▐▹ Because of their unique body shapes, wildly disparate sizes, and intriguing colorations, animals offer the logo designer plenty of creative options. (All designs created by Gardner Design.)

TOP DOWN: Wichita Montessori School, SeaWorld BlueTeam, Books for Life, Bradley Paper

:• Animals have always figured prominently in the minds of humans. In the past, animals were a source of resources—food, furs, and transportation among them—but also a source of danger. (Petroglyphs at Newspaper Rock, Indian Creek, Utah)

MYTHOLOGICAL CREATURES

We are a society of storytellers. We love stories. We use stories as a tool to sell our heritage, morals, and ethos to our children. In many of these stories, mythological creatures figure prominently. Think Little Mermaid. Think Big Bad Wolf. Think Batman.

The mythological creature is even more malleable than a real one. It can have special powers or bizarre qualities. A horse is good, yes, but what if it had wings? A horn? Is it pure white or black or multicolored? What if it could talk or fight valiantly? It just gets more and more interesting.

For all their diversity, the mythological creatures included in this collection have two common traits: All could be said to be alive, at least in the imagination, and all have a story connected to them. When we already know that story, the path to discovering the meaning of a myth-based logo is short.

Some of these creatures are known worldwide. For example, the use of skeletons or skulls in identifiers such as flags or banners goes back to pirate flags of the 1700s. As a symbol of death or danger, it is almost universally understood.

But others are not so widely understood, and unless such a reference only needs to be understood within a specific geographic area or group, its use in a logo should be carefully considered.

For example, consider the witch Baba Yaga, the central character in a Slavic tale who lures children to her home. Her house has giant chicken legs that carry it about in the forest and so can never be found in the same place. Baba Yaga flies about in a mortar and pestle, and like most witches, is a horrible hag. But in some versions of her story, if a visitor is kind, polite, and/or wise, Baba Yaga provides invaluable answers to questions—but every answer she gives ages her another year.

Clearly, the story is rich in visual and emotional triggers. But if Baba Yaga is not a story that you grew up with, it is very difficult to relate to it, at least at first telling. Even the most adeptly designed logo that includes a house on chicken legs or an old woman sitting in a pestle will be meaningless—or just plain crazy—to all but those who heard the story as children and have since contextualized its meaning as adults.

We may be becoming a more homogeneous people in terms of our commercial lives and products, but in some respects, local cultures are much slower to change. Myths just don't cross cultural boundaries well.

▶ Standing atop a tall column in Piccadilly Circus in London, the Eros statue is symbolic of how integrated mythology is in modern society. It is of us and around us, but of a higher nature.

But mythological references can be dangerous in logos even within a single country or region. Not even neighbors know the same stories: For example, in the United States, many Native Americans are familiar with stories of Coyote, the trickster, who gets himself in scrape after scrape. But move outside of those families, even within the same grade school, and Coyote is completely unknown.

There are also situations where a certain area's mental picture of a mythological creature differs from that of other areas. A spirit or ghost might appear in the mind of one person as a sheet-covered, floating shape, as a malevolent, ragged wretch to another, or as a semitranspar-ent human or animal form to yet another person. The word *ghost* simply does not conjure up a consistent image.

Cultural references are also shifting. The visual portrayal of a vampire in the eighteenth century is markedly different from the movie vampire of today. At one time, they were portrayed as the evil and ugly undead. Today, they can be young, attractive, and quite sympathetic characters.

Stories today are very often illustrated through media, so mythological creatures can be cartoon or anime characters. In the future, will the Wii mini-Mii be a meaningful character? Bart Simpson? The GEICO gecko? It's hard to know now what will gain traction over time.

The common thread of using mythological characters in a logo design is that it pulls up the viewer's past through story and memory, and connects it to the present. It draws people into the identity using the knowledge they already have.

ARCHETYPES

Aristotle believed that we increase our knowledge by employing the knowledge we already have of the archetype. From our understanding of the ideal example springs appreciation of related facts. If a rabbit is fast, and the logo for a delivery company includes a rabbit, then the company offers fast delivery.

Animals and mythological creatures are, in many ways, the perfect archetypes. Once we understand what a rabbit is, it's a short hop to abstract that knowledge and apply it to something else—a courier, a Christian holiday, soft porn, you name it. It's only a matter of how convincing that logo can be.

—Bill Gardner, LogoLounge.com

(Note: The mythology section of this book is quite diverse and contains some figures that might be controversial. In particular, there are Christ representations in this section, but we are not implying that Christ is mythological. Also, robots actually exist, although you will find robots in this section, too.

For purposes of categorization, the word "mythological" is used here to describe anything you would not normally see coming down the street today on its own power. Each entity in this section displays some signs of being alive in the present.)

∴ Each of these designs has a base in mythology, but it's not necessary to know the actual story in order to appreciate the logo and what it represents. (All designs created by Gardner Design.)

TOP DOWN: AmeriMerc Pool Supply, Advanced Retail E-Commerce System (ARES), Reno Technology Manufacturing

Tracy Sabin *has worked as a well-respected designer and illustrator for more than 25 years. His cache of awards and portfolio of client work is significant (see www.sabingrafik. com), but perhaps even more noteworthy is his ability to connect to the ultimate viewer. Much of his logo design is purely illustrative, each creation sharing an intriguing story about the client. He speaks here about how and why creatures of all sorts populate his designs.*

Why do you think animals come up so frequently in logos/identity systems?

⠶ People generally like animals and find them interesting. You want a logo to be memorable and to elicit positive reactions, so it's not a surprise that the category of animals would be among the most used image classes in logos.

Animals are fascinating. They have unique characteristics and they go about their lives in idiosyncratic ways, shaped by the niche they occupy. Humans have a rich history with animals in folklore and the myriad human/animal interactions, so there is a deep source of associated concepts to draw from when working with animal imagery.

Do you think that animals, as living beings that are imbued with some personality and specific physical attributes and abilities, are more intriguing to the human mind than are other humans? Why or why not?

⠶ Animals may carry less baggage than human imagery. It's also often easier to represent a particular attribute using an animal. Peter Oehjne of Eiche, Oehjne Design art-directed me to explore images of a charging rhino for a German public relations firm. I believe his thinking was that this was a good way to represent the hard-charging, can't-ignore-it communications that the firm developed to promote its clients. The idea of using a rhino to represent a PR firm may seem a bit odd, but it's arresting and hopefully it's a good fit with the attributes of the company. I think it's important that there is a fit. Without it, an animal representing a company can just seem arbitrary.

> # Animals may carry less baggage than human imagery. It's also often easier to represent a particular attribute **using an animal.** ⠶

Certain animal attributes could be considered trite and somewhat tiresome: Brave as a lion. Clever as a you-know-what. But in a logo, these clichés are used again and again. Why does triteness work in these cases?

⠶ Generally, people need to "get" a logo on a first viewing, so the use of clichés is essential. As you point out, clichés carry with them the risk of triteness that is not a good attribute for a logo. A common way to exploit the quick associations of a cliché and at the same time neutralize the triteness is to add an unexpected twist to the

1

2

1: Beithan Hessler Corporate Communications
2: Brown Deer Press

BROWN DEER
PRESS

image. When we were developing the logo for Brown Deer Press, it was a given that a brown deer would be part of the logo. The art director, Ron Miriello of Miriello Grafico, saw a way to add a twist to the image by turning the antlers into branches. Books are made from trees, so there is a tenuous logic in this marriage of disparate concepts, and people find it memorable.

In your logo work, animals appear frequently. Why do they appeal to you (excepting examples like Brown Deer Press, which suggests a visual)?

▪ Broadly speaking, I think there needs to be some logical connection to the identity even if it's not implied in the company name. For several years I developed logos for a medical convention for heart specialists that took place in different tropical locations. The art director, Scott Mires of

Felix Sockwell on Republicrat

As told by Felix Sockwell, Maplewood, New Jersey

"In 'Political Animosity,' which is a visually driven essay published in *The Chicago Tribune* a week before the 2008 election on the history of the donkey and elephant symbols penned by Thomas Nast in 1870, I provided a quick rundown of everything we've seen since. Basically, it is a history and critique of the party logos. The symbol I came up with is a combination.

"This was the first time anyone published one of my logo rants in a large publication. The particular solution isn't exactly mind-blowing, but it's kind of funny and a fast read.

"In the months before the election, the Democratic Party decided to ditch the image of the donkey altogether in favor of a generic Denver skyline. The Republicans chose a conservative, yet aggressively postured elephant. Why either party made such decisions or how they actually affected the result is up for debate. But there is no question that the 'O' logo turned out to be one of the most impressive and landmark identities ever seen—and sold." ▪

3

4

5

3, 4, 5: The Masters Group event

MiresBall, suggested I explore ideas in which tropical aquatic animals are arranged in the shape of a heart. One year, it was sea horses, another year angelfish, a third year, mermaids. Again, we exploited the combination of two unrelated concepts to create a surprising image that tells the story of the event in a succinct way.

What is your favorite animal to include in an identity and why?

▪▪ I try not to have a favorite animal. The type of animal is best suggested by the "logo problem." Craig Fuller from Greenhaus suggested I try some nest and egg images for a new housing development. The development was located in a natural environment with lots of wildlife and beautiful vistas. In addition to the association with nature, I think Craig liked some of the other associations we make with a nest. We even refer to "nesting" in our homes and we like to think of it as a place to nurture and protect our families. The animal used—an unborn bird, which itself implies new beginnings and possibilities for the future—sprang naturally from reflections about this particular development.

For a while, I used the image of a pug in my own identity. I owned a pug at the time. Eventually I abandoned the image because it felt too arbitrary.

Can you name an animal logo design of your own that is a particular favorite? Why do you think it is successful for the client?

▪▪ I was pretty happy with the Soil Reliever logo (page 17), art-directed by Doug Powell of Farm-Links. The company manufactures devices that golf courses use to aerate the sod. They utilize the longest and least destructive tines in the industry. I used a stylized panther with exaggerated, exposed claws to symbolize what their product delivers. The image also conveys the concepts of power and precision, and it's memorable.

On the subject of mythology: These figures are highly symbolic and highly charged. Why do humans respond to them so strongly?

▪▪ They are a part of our culture, and the stories that surround them are familiar and can therefore be exploited by a logo designer. I think there is a fantasy aspect to these strange creatures that appeals to people. We like to envision an existence that is unbounded by the normal constraints we experience.

These figures also have a high degree of magic or sometimes make-believe surrounding them. How does this work in favor of a logo? How could it work against?

CANYON HILLS

Sabingrafik
INCORPORATED

Gianluigi Tobanelli on A. J. Mobilità Sri

As told by Gianluigi Tobanelli, Studio GT&P, Foligno, Italy

"An animal as a logo can become almost a totemic symbol that protects and inspires the company's activities. For A. J. Mobilità Sri, a new Italian company headquartered in Spoleto that manages municipality and private parking areas with advanced electronic detection systems that help customers find available parking places, a flying seagull represented the company activity.

"It is a symbol of freedom and movement, flying high to optimize the city's mobility and improving citizens' freedom of movement. To give it a sense of movement, it was made to be slightly out-of-focus, as if it were always flying.

"A logo is successful if it is original; it has to stand out and must not be confused with others. It must be simple and straightforward, but at the same time must not be trivial. It has to have its own personality and raise interest in who is looking at it. These are features which I believe the A. J. logo owns." ❖

6: Canyon Hills logo, **7:** Sabingrafik Incorporated logo,
8 & 9: Sensa logo trial and final

Figures that foster a dream of a better life can be a good fit with mythological imagery. I used a mermaid image for a plastic surgery clinic located along the Pacific Ocean. There is the ocean connection as well as the mesmerizing beauty and exoticness one associates with a mermaid.

At what point does a mythological reference become too oblique for the wider audience to understand?

Unfortunately, I think the general population is less familiar with folktales and myths than in previous generations. That diminishes the power of associations for these images. Knowledge of the persona (or lack thereof) is definitely a factor in deciding whether to use a particular image or not.

Do you think that the disappearance of folktales and myths is a worldwide situation?

To some extent, the centuries-old tales and myths have been supplanted by the licensed characters of the mass media era—Batman, Transformers, Disney characters, etc. These are the myths and folktales of our age and, because they are proprietary, they are not directly available to designers for inspiration. I think this is a fairly worldwide phenomenon, though less media-oriented societies may have more contact with the old stories.

On the other side of the coin, people have accepted the Nike symbol quite easily (although the reference to the winged foot may have been lost from the start). Is it crucial that the viewer understand all of the symbolism?

Not necessarily. The Nike logo works more because of its simplicity and dynamic movement than because of its associations to mythology. I'm sure many people are unaware of the connection. I think also that a logo can gain in

stature because of its association with the product or entity it represents. Nike has done such a good job building its brand that the consumer perception of the logo shape and the product it represents have become indivisible.

Is it dangerous to use a mythical reference for a logo when it might not be understood, especially if the client's business grows outside of its original area?

I think that's generally true. If you don't know that Atlas, punished by Zeus, was required to hold up the celestial sphere for all eternity, then you may not appreciate the desired message in Turner Entertainment's icon, designed for a promotion, that the company is responsible for a large and important archive of films and that this responsibility rests firmly on their shoulders, so to speak. Fortunately, some stories remain familiar and our global economy may actually be extending some of the stories to a larger audience.

Could you name a favorite mythology-based logo that you especially like?

The Starbucks logo, which uses a mermaid, is clearly a success, providing another example in which the mark and the product it represents have been carefully built in tandem to become one of today's dominant brands. The connection between a mermaid and coffee may not be clear to the average user but this pairing of concepts is unique and appealing.

I am partial to pictorial logos, partly because I am a visually oriented person and partly because I believe that people naturally relate to pictures more than abstractions. The current Starbucks logo is particular enough in its rendering to be memorable while sufficiently simplified to work as a logo and to hold up in its many types of reproductions. That can be a hard balance.

10

11

12

13

10: Soil Reliever, 11: Coastal Plastic Surgery, 12: Turner Entertainment, 13: University of California, San Diego

Naughtyfish

Paul Garbett on Naughtyfish

As told by Paul Garbett of Naughtyfish, Sydney, Australia

"Naughtyfish is something my brother Carl and I said to each other as children. We liked the image of a fish that would swim against the current and not follow the school. When he passed away in 1999, I wanted to keep his spirit alive, so I used that for the company name. When we were establishing our studio, we decided we would only do it if we could pursue the work we wanted. Today that's what we do.

"Our logo depicts another story behind our name: Millions of years ago, when all life was in the water, there was a fish who wanted to experience life on land. Slowly, he began to develop limbs and, over time, became one of the first land-dwelling animals. It is the spirit of that recalcitrant fish we celebrate.

"The origin of our logo and name is one of the most common questions we get. Once people hear the story, they get it. The logo is interactive as it compels people to find out about it. It also seems to act as a kind of filter so that people who do approach us seem to be open to our way of thinking."

Credits: Designers: Paul Garbett, Danielle de Andrade

Andreas Karl *runs his own graphic design studio, Karl Design, in Vienna, Austria. He is a prolific logo designer and is also quite involved with design for humanitarian and environmental projects. Although his design for the Euro coin received millions of votes in a public referendum and was clearly selected as the preferred design, it was ultimately not chosen by the politicians. His ability to secure both meaning and art in a contained space, such as the Euro coin or a logo, makes him a favorite with many clients.*

What makes animals so emblematic to the human mind?

:• Since the beginning of mankind, humans have drawn animals. The paintings in the cave of Lascaux in southwestern France, for example, are estimated to be more than 16,000 years old. We see realistic images of horses, cattle, bison, felines, birds, bears, rhinoceros, and big-horned bulls. Animals lived on this Earth long before man.

A well-done animal logo can be as strong as a good abstract logo, like the Nike swoosh, the peace sign, or the Mercedes-Benz symbol, because every child comes to know and love animals. If we hear World Wildlife Federation, we instantly have a black-and-white giant panda in mind.

In Germany, Switzerland, and Austria, where I live today, you don't see logos with animals very often. Most of the product and company brands use prosaic lettering, unemotional initials, or abstract symbolism. Kindergartens, zoos, or the ecology movement sometimes show an animal in their logos.

Why are humans so fascinated with animals?

:• Look at insects and birds, for example: They are much smaller than we are, but they can fly by their own power. Look at the biggest mammals on Earth: Whales easily dive down to 6,000 feet (1,829 m). Look at the land turtles on the Galapagos Islands. Some of them can live over 250 years. These animals have our respect because they are superior to us in a certain manner.

Many humans don't live in or with nature but in cultivated areas like towns and big cities, surrounded by concrete and noise, and often in overpopulated areas. Woods and large-scale parks are scarce commodities. So there are some people who rarely see a colorful butterfly, a nicely striped poison snake, or a rhino. I guess that's the reason why we learn a pictogram of an animal much easier and faster than a pictogram of a car, a skyscraper, or a woman with a baby carriage.

> # Since the beginning of mankind, humans have **drawn animals.** :•

Are some animals easier to relate to?

:• If I'm doing a logo with an animal in it, I always try to put a focus on a certain attribute or a gesture. I want an animal to look proud or wise, noble or powerful—but always friendly and sympathetic. And this works better with animals

1

2

3

4

1: Fantastic Windsurfing, **2:** Solutions Hamburg, **3:** Adler
Apotheke Dachsbach, **4:** Enterfox Marketing Group

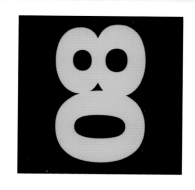

Bradford Lawton on the San Antonio ZooBall Gala

As told by Bradford Lawton of The Bradford Lawton Design Group, San Antonio, Texas

"The San Antonio Zoo approached us about creating an overall identity for its 2008 ZooBall gala, its biggest fund-raising event of the year. The theme was 'Monkey Business,' which didn't really inspire us. It was hard to not stray into referring to the Marx Brothers film or doing something campy. No directions were exciting.

"To get 'unstuck' I just started drawing to see what would come. Still not feeling like it was going anywhere, I took a break. When I came back, I happened to view my sketches from the side, and the '08' appeared. It's one of those solutions where you feel like didn't create it—it was handed to you.

"I've always felt there were three levels of solutions. The first is the kind where if you gave the same problem to ten designers, three would come up with it—a good solution, but nothing that special. The second kind blows the other nine away. And the third is something more spiritual, like you were just the conduit. That's what this design was." ⠶

Credits: CD: Bradford Lawton; Designers: Bradford Lawton, Josh Zapata; Acct. supervisor: Lindsay Crowell

that have a face with big visible eyes such as a horse, a cat, or an eagle. In my logos, animals must never look aggressive or threatening. Aggressiveness, danger, or ugliness have no business in logo design.

Do you have a favorite animal?

▪ All animals are beautiful, even hairy spiders. But it is not so much a certain animal that I like, more like a part of an animal: wings. I like wings and feathers in nearly all variations. Don't ask me why. Maybe because they have a deep mythological meaning and some kind of expression of freedom or flying away from trouble. They lift the theme up in another dimension, make a logo look lighter, more dynamic, and visionary in some way. Airlines often use winged logos, and some car companies like Chrysler and BMW for their Mini. The logos of Bentley and Aston Martin are two of my favorites.

The logo for my own design studio is a winged Taurus. It is a combination of my horoscope and the mythological tale of Europa and the bull. God Zeus fell in love with Europa, the daughter of King Agenor of Phoenicia. In the ancient world, immortal gods could not simply meet with mortal humans on the street or sit together in a nice Greek restaurant. So Zeus disguised himself as a handsome bull to come closer to his love. Europa, who was playing on the beach with the other girls of Tyre, was entranced by this beautiful creature and climbed on its back. The bull began to paddle in the surf and she became alarmed when the Taurus began to swim strongly out to sea. By now, Europa had realized that this was no ordinary bull. Both arrived at the Crete shore, where Zeus revealed his true identity and seduced Europa. Instead of a woman's figure I gave my Taurus wings, symbolizing that it is not just any bull.

Please describe a favorite animal-based logo that you created.

▪ Once I did a logo with a seahorse for a classical music event on a riverboat (page 23). The form of its spiral tail follows the form of a clef. I like this combination a lot. In my opinion, this logo is a good fit to the client's concerts. Seahorses are graceful little animals. Very fragile on the one hand and artificial on the other—same as instruments for classical music.

As far as animal logos created by other people are concerned, the NBC Peacock logo, redesigned by Chermayeff & Geismar in 1986, is one of my absolute favorites. This logo is and will be a benchmark in identity design and was always a great inspiration for my own work.

Why does mythology resonate so strongly within the human mind?

▪ Why do we like *Harry Potter*, *Lord of the Rings*, *Tomb Raider*, or other modern fairy tales? The protagonists in these stories use superpowers, and who doesn't want to have superpowers? I like the dragon logo Heinz Edelmann did for the German publisher Klett-Cotta. And Agip, the oil company with the six-footed lion [logo], proclaims in its ads: *Wir reissen uns sechs Beine für Sie aus*, which literally means, "We tear out our six legs for you," making it known they go to great effort to satisfy their clients.

We always want the opposite of what we have. If we see our lives to be frustrating or boring, we want to escape and flee into fantasy worlds where we are happy, strong, or rich. In the past, Roman gods played an important role in daily life. They were seen as powerful, omnipotent, and immortal. A Roman and Greek citizen's lifeline and luck was dependent on the grace of the gods.

5

6

7

8

5: Deute-Fahr Landmaschinen, 6: Initiative Verfossungs-Referendum, 7: Ethianum Klink Heidelberg, 8: Karl Design Vienna

Eric Ruffing and Dave Parmley on X Games

As told by Eric Ruffing and Dave Parmley, principals of 13THFLOOR, San Juan Capistrano, California

"There are three categories of skulls: evil and satanic, which we don't do—we will go to the edge of the abyss but don't fall in. Then you have funky, cool skulls—playful and hip but not for kids. Then you have juvenile skulls.

"This design was created for use on an X Games fingerboard/skateboard. The demographic is boys age 5 to 9, and market testing had shown that they wanted more skulls. Skulls and crosses are core to the skater world, but combining the core iron cross with the funkier skull gave kids a fresh option from the more typical 'death skulls' already seen on a lot of deck art.

"We wanted to keep the execution loose and nutty in attitude, so it's all done in pencil. It's as if a kid drew it himself on the margin of his notebook while bored to tears in math class. There's a million ways to do skulls: They're not just cold bone. The idea is to give each its own personality and something the client can own."

Credits: CD: Roman Cortez; AD, design, art: 13THFLOOR

How do people of different cultures relate to mythological symbols from other people?

▪ The swastika, for example, is one of the oldest mythological symbols still existing. It is a sacred and prehistoric symbol for the highest knowledge of mankind. It is also a symbol of the expanding galaxies and universes for the relative sphere of life. On Japanese and Chinese maps you can find it as a symbol for a holy temple or a shrine. For the people of the San Blas Islands at the coast of Panama, the swastika symbolizes a four-armed octopus. They use it as the central design element on their national flag.

But in Germany it is forbidden by law to use a swastika (or *Hakenkreuz*) in the public. It has a very negative connotation and every German schoolkid learns why.

Some weeks ago, I visited Rome and strolled through the old city center without a plan. On my way I ended up in front of a toy store. At the entrance stood a big wooden Pinocchio figure, at least seven feet tall. Inside the little shop you could find hundreds of Pinocchios of all different kinds: Bigger ones and very tiny ones, wooden or plastic, cheap stuff from China, and very expensive handcrafted rarities. Every figure had a long nose. We all know the story behind it: With every lie he told, Pinocchio's nose grew longer and longer.

I haven't used this fairy tale for a logo yet, but upon returning to Vienna I saw a funnel shaped like the face of Pinocchio in the window of a kitchen store. Funny to see how modern design and old childhood fables can melt together in an efficient combination, to a new innovation.

Can mythological references in logo design become too historically distant or oblique for people to understand?

▪ I don't think it is necessary for the success of a brand that everybody understands the idea or the symbolic language behind a company or product logo. It is more important that the logo itself as a unique form sinks into the memory of the viewer and gets well known in the public. Ninety-nine percent of the German people do not know the meaning and heritage of the Mercedes-Benz emblem or the logo of the Deutsche Bank, one of the biggest finance companies in the world. But this ignorance is no disadvantage for the popularity of these brands or the success of the companies behind the symbol. In my own perception, the audience is less critical as we, as brand designers, often think they might be. Most consumers don't ask, "What is this logo all about?" or "Why is it blue?" They accept it as a given after a while and get used to it.

But a logo can have too much mythology in it. When I worked as a creative director at FCB/Design in Frankfurt, we did a redesign for a pharmaceutical company named Spitzner. The company had an old logo showing a simply drawn unicorn with an earring jumping over a mountain ridge. The whole sketch was surrounded by a circle. Nobody could tell me what the picture or its symbolism represented. The only thing I knew: The logo was totally overcharged with elements, so I decided to reduce it to the unicorn's head. The client liked the idea.

What is key to ensuring that a mythologically based logo works?

▪ Tracy Sabin of Sabingrafik designed a very nice logo for the University of California, San Diego sports team, the Tritons (www.ucsdtritons.com). It shows a Greek god standing in the waves and throwing his trident. I especially like the way Tracy did the face and the muscles. It is a perfect and convincing play of light and shadow and a high-professional illustration with a powerful expression, not often seen in sports. (See the logo on page 17.)

9

10

11

12

9: Flying Foxes women's basketball team, 10: Chelly Catfood, 11: Riverboat Classics, 12: Spitzner Arzeimittel

Von Glitschka on Street Value

As told by Von Glitschka, Salem, Oregon

"Street Value is run by two Americans living in Hong Kong. They sell urban culture wear—clothing, gadgets, anything that appeals to the urban street market. They wanted to get into the vinyl toy market.

"Originally, the clients wanted me to do a DJ-type character. I started with a monster DJ—kind of a cyclops with lots of bling and a turntable. I ran those sketches by them, but by then, they decided they didn't want a DJ. So I wiggled around with it some more, and this monster emerged.

"The squid cyclops is just a fun guy. It is rendered in a cute style, so anyone will like him.

"The great thing about working on these sorts of designs is that no one is going to rip on me for not getting the tentacles right or anything like that. I just did a poster for Adobe with this little worm who is smoking a pipe and speaking Japanese. That kind of thing is fine when you're creating make-believe creatures.

Michael Vanderbyl *is dean of design of California College of the Arts. He established Vanderbyl Design in 1973 and has since gone on to work in many fields of design, most recently in furniture retail spaces. An acclaimed speaker and winner of dozens of design awards, Vanderbyl is known for his figurative, storytelling logos, many of which have survived well for decades.*

Why do animals spark the creative mind like they do?

▪▪ Often, animals come to mind on a logo project because they are integral to the subject. For instance, it would be hard to do a logo for Coyote Books without using a coyote.

But animals are figurative elements that people relate to. They're friendly, even when we show them as ferocious animals. The Cardinals football team has this ferocious-looking bird logo, but it still cracks me up.

Animals also end up serving as metaphors for the human condition. Pixar has lots of movies like this, starring fish or panda bears. They take the place of humans and their various traits, and human viewers are more accepting of them. Animals aren't politicized; they are neutral. Especially in logos, you don't want something that is already politicized or culturally off-putting.

Using an animal in a logo brings things to a different plane, a more neutral place.

I also think that animals, for the most part, are thought of fondly by people. Almost everyone has seen animals in nature or at the zoo, or they have pets. So including an animal creates a safe place. The designer is the one who adds the personality that is unique to the project.

Animals also have interesting shapes that are so much more engaging than the human shape. We tend to view them from the side, not the front as we do when we picture people. The face is the way into getting to know a person; body shape is how we get to know animals.

Why are we so prone to turn animals into symbols?

▪▪ A lot of animals already have a symbolic nature—tenacity or sweetness, for example. We just take that nature and build on it. Puma, as a brand, has done that very well. The actual animal is sleek and fast, and therefore the logo based on it successfully reflects the product.

> # You just have to consider very carefully all of the attributes of an animal before you **include it in a design.** ▪▪

A logo that I created and still like a lot is for the California Conservation Corps. Basically, the Corps' mission is to conserve natural resources for future generations. I took a graphical version of a mother brown bear—the brown bear is the state animal of California—and created a cub out of the negative space in her body.

This logo became a symbol for protection of natural resources for future generations. It tied

1

2

1: Coyote Books logo
2: California Conservation Corps logo

the mythology of the bear to the generational care of the mother toward the cub.

Another logo that does this quite well is the World Wildlife Federation. It is very nicely resolved, using an animal that is friendly and rare. It's a great symbol.

Are there times when using an animal can be dangerous?

Usually this relates to the client. We created a logo for a wine called Wildass, and we had to use a donkey in the logo so that people didn't think we were being obscene.

Benjamin Franklin wanted the turkey to be the national bird of the United States. That would have been pretty odd today. Turkeys aren't regarded as independent, beautiful birds at all. They might be fast or crafty, but they're certainly

Nico A. Pranoto on Little Taipei

As told by Nico A. Pranoto, AD/CD of Banana, Inc., Indonesia

"For Little Taipei, a new restaurant in a Jakarta mall, our client wanted to combine a traditional Chinese menu with a more modern fast-food approach—you wait in line to order and pay before seated, which was a challenge because the typical Asian audience was not familiar with this concept when they are looking for Chinese food.

"We finally came up with a teenage dragon with sleek curves and an uncluttered outline. It characterized the younger generation; its open mouth symbolized spicy foods and gave him a smiley articulation. We included the hard-edged chopsticks to show nontraditional fast food and a simple plate, instead of the old-fashioned bowl. A bamboo font was altered to associate more modernity.

"For the brand's expression, perfect solutions came from the icon. Posters displayed dramatic close-ups of the dragon's hands. Repeat patterns of small dragons populate the restaurant walls. He's a dragon that really rocks."

Credits: CD/AD: Nico A. Pranoto; Illustrator: Popo

not all that an eagle is. You just have to consider very carefully all of the attributes of an animal before you include it in a design.

I am always more fond of a figurative form, more so than a random geometry. A figure has more personality and life. I think most Americans like animals more as well. We like stories that we can understand right away. Maybe we use animals in the same way that heraldry is used in other parts of the world. Maybe they are just modern heraldry.

What is the role of myth in design?

When design functions best, it is about a narrative. It should be telling a story. That story allows the audience to connect to the client's service or product.

Sometimes it's harder to tell that story. I had a client called the American Center of Wine, Food and the Arts. For a designer, a name like that strikes fear into your heart: How am I going to represent all of this? I thought about the bonding connection food has to people all over the world. It both sustains life and can present some of the highest experiences in life. The client has a cultural aspect, too. It holds cultural and art exhibitions, so I really couldn't just show a turkey leg and a bottle of wine.

Although it wasn't asked for in the brief, I decided to explore mythology to figure it out. I honed in on Copia, the goddess of abundance, as in "cornucopia." She was one of Bacchus's fellow gods. Instead of being pedantic and showing a knife and fork, for example, I raised it to a higher level and created a logo with a nude woman nurturing a grapevine. Years after I did that logo, the museum called and said they had decided to change its name to just "Copia."

Mythology was definitely the answer in that case. It alluded very easily to a larger cultural idea, but still works as a nurturing image even if you don't know about Copia.

Why do people like myths so much?

> ⋮ They give us a way of explaining things we don't understand, such as ships crashing because mermaids lured sailors toward the rocks.

All stories and the characters in them are a way for humans to justify a phenomenon or narrative that really exists but which doesn't have the facts to back it up. Think about Thor, the god of thunder. He was here long before we understood unstable atmospheric conditions.

Myths don't always travel that well, though. I remember doing a logo for a nonprofit educational foundation. I drew a man and woman in silhouette with olive-branch wreaths on their heads. It got rejected because the foundation said that it was a Western perspective of representing education, and that it wouldn't be relevant to African or Asian cultures.

Or take the example of Copia. When you do things like show a nude woman, portraying her as she would have been as a god, you have to wonder how the client will accept that. The client

Evgeny Golovach on Minin & Pojarskiy

As told by Evgeny Golovach of Redbrand, Moscow, Russia

"Minin & Pojarskiy is a new Russian clothing brand. Its distinguishing feature is casual clothing that has elements of country and military style.

"The bear is a very important symbol for all Russian people. Many Russian tales, legends, and proverbs include the bear. It means strength, force, endurance, and courage—a very positive image. The bear is also the most recognizable symbol of Russia in the larger world. We wanted to draw attention to the brand's origin and the strong, positive energy. We also wanted the logo to be nonstandard for the fashion industry, without repeating existing tendencies.

"The main inspiration for the font design was ancient Russian tales and Lubok graphics. Using this face created a modern logo with a Russian theme, which is reflected in the Cyrillic version (not shown here)." ⋮

4

3: Wildass Wine identity,
4: Copia

5: Coqui logo and identity extension, **6:** Scarecrow Wine logo

was a woman, so she was fine with it. But a man might have been more cautious and objected.

Those are cases in which a myth can get you into trouble—when you violate some politically correct aspect.

Do you ever worry about people not understanding a myth-based logo?

It's all about the narrative in which the logo is shown. You can't just put up some design with nothing around it and rely on people to know the story. It's the implementation that helps explain.

Batman is an extremely strong myth, and its logo is extremely strong. It's one of those logos and stories that has, probably unfortunately, infiltrated the world. It's surrounded with marketing and publicity.

Nike is a different sort of case. The student who created the Nike logo way back when probably never dreamed it would ever go on a shoe, much less be so famous. It was just created for a contest. The Nike logo pops the balloon, as far as I'm concerned, of all this Pepsi-logo-instant-justification kind of thing, with all the heavy brand-speak. The Nike logo was made exceptional over time through its implementation.

Sometimes, if a viewer doesn't know the story behind a logo, it almost works to your advantage. It's like when you see an optical illusion drawing. When you "get it," it draws you in one more level. The viewer becomes connected to the logo in a way that they wouldn't have before.

You've had the opportunity to work with lots of students over the years. Do they have a wider or more limited understanding of myth today?

Students today haven't been steeped in the European minimalism that I was, and they are also living in an era of "shiny." Their education is not as dogmatic as mine was, nor do they have to create logos that are faced with all kinds of production challenges, such as the ability to print it on a pen or a billboard. So they tend to the more figurative and even cartoony.

They are far more figurative than abstract. They put faces on things a lot and are more expressive. They think more in terms of animation. It's certainly not the Bauhaus anymore.

But there are practicalities to this. We did a logo for a water park that showed this croaking frog. Instead of creating just one logo, we created three, showing him in three different positions.

So he's "animated" in the sense that he has three different moves that the client can use.

Can you describe a favorite myth-based logo from your office?

▪▸ Scarecrow Wine is a great client. The owner of this winery is the grandson of the former head of the MGM movie company when it created Wizard of Oz. We needed something that was friendly and didn't violate copyrights.

I like this logo because of the story behind it, and I like the positive–negative nature of it. It has a lot of personality, but it's still steeped in classic European design, with the two ovals forming the negative space for the face.

As a designer, you are always looking for a built-in vocabulary to tap into, something that offers personality and life.

Thomas Vasquez on Centaur

As told by Thomas Vasquez, Brooklyn, New York

"This identity is for a company that's no longer around called Hair Products For Men. The intention here was to create an image that spoke to and exemplified the type of audience we were trying to attract: men in their late teens on up to their early 30s.

"The type of image I decided to go with was really based on the product name: Centaur pomade. The angular look of the logo, along with the feeling of movement, muscular strength, weaponry, and stylization, all lent to the overall feeling of a smooth, masculine, fashion-based product for men.

"I incorporated the letter C as a visual representation of the bow that was traditionally carried by this mythological creature for hunting and battle, which are also ancient symbols of masculinity. My inspiration was derived from the bold, graphic look of images painted onto ancient Greek pottery." ▪▸

6

animals

A **B** **C**

1

2

3

4

D = Design Firm **C** = Client

1A **D** Studio Simon **C** Golden Baseball League 1B **D** Sayles Graphic Design, Inc. **C** Iowa Vets 1C **D** Greteman Group

2A **D** Glitschka Studios **C** Federal Bureau of Illustration 2B **D** julian peck **C** Guardian Bells 2C **D** Art Chantry **C** King of Hawaii

3A **D** stressdesign **C** STRAC Tech 3B **D** Truly Design **C** Porcaputtana streetwear 3C **D** Eagle Imagery **C** Eagle Imagery

4A **D** Hoyne Design **C** Foster's Australia 4B **D** Rickabaugh Graphics **C** Hasbro 4C **D** GMMB **C** USA Freedom Corps

A **B** **C**

   **1**

   **2**

   **3**

   **4**

D = Design Firm **C** = Client

1A **D** Glitschka Studios **C** Tactix Creative   1B **D** The Logo Factory, Inc.   **C** Grand PAC   1C **D** POLLARDdesign **C** Nike

2A **D** Thelogoloft.com   **C** Republic Danger Industries   2B **D** Velocity Design Group   **C** Made Safe Investigation   2C **D** 2TREES DESIGN   **C** 2TREES DESIGN

3A **D** Alphabet Arm Design   **C** Kay Hanley   3B **D** DUSTIN PARKER ARTS   **C** American Builders   3C **D** Rocketman Creative   **C** CAD CAM Southwest

4A **D** XY ARTS   **C** Greek Orthodox Church of Mentone & Districts   4B **D** Brian Blankenship   4C **D** Extraverage Productions   **C** Personal

A **B** **C**

1

2

3

4

D = Design Firm **C** = Client

1A **D** Ryan Cooper Design **C** Dave Hall 1B **D** Pat Taylor, Inc. **C** Phoenix Park Hotel 1C **D** Lysergid **C** Loïc SATTLER

2A **D** Rickabaugh Graphics **C** IUP 2B **D** Rickabaugh Graphics **C** Northeastern State 2C **D** Rickabaugh Graphics **C** Fresno Pacific University

3A **D** Barnstorm Creative Group Inc **C** Burrard International 3B **D** X-ist **C** Wesley Clark Campaign 3C **D** Sharisse Steber Design **C** Jade Eagle Security, LTD

4A **D** Artnak **C** Oru 4B **D** Q **C** Argus 4C **D** Vigor Creative, Inc. **C** self promotion

	A	**B**	**C**	
1				
2				
3				
4				

D = Design Firm   **C** = Client

1A **D** Gardner Design **C** Roosevelt's Restaurant   1B **D** Squires and Company **C** Baggage Cart of America   1C **D** Lienhart Design **C** Heritage Bank
2A **D** DUEL Purpose **C** Starrland, Inc.   2B **D** J6Studios **C** International Aikido Association   2C **D** Double Brand **C** Marshal's Office of the Wielkopolska Region in Poznan
3A **D** Candor Advertising **C** Candor Advertising   3B **D** RedBrand **C** SkyPatrol   3C **D** Spark Studio **C** MotorOne
4A **D** Glitschka Studios **C** Air Power   4B **D** Tactix Creative **C** Work, Inc.   4C **D** Stiles Design **C** Republic National Distributing Co.

A

B

C

1

2

3

4

D = Design Firm **C** = Client

1A **D** Jon Flaming Design **C** Arrington Oil & Gas 1B **D** Greteman Group 1C **D** TracyLocke Dallas **C** Huffman Elementary School

2A **D** RARE Design **C** University of Southern Mississippi 2B **D** CVAD_CommunicationDesign **C** University of North Texas

2C **D** Squires and Company **C** Baggage Cart of America 3A **D** Karl Design Vienna **C** Delikatessen / Dortmunder Brauerei

3B **D** Rickabaugh Graphics **C** Louisiana University, Monroe 3C **D** Glitschka Studios **C** Tactix Creative 4A **D** Steele Design **C** Eastman Outfitters

4B **D** Graphic D-Signs, Inc. **C** American Landscaping & Construction Services 4C **D** Design Coup Inc. **C** Falcon Solutions

 A

 B

 C 1

   2

   3

   4

Ⓓ = Design Firm Ⓒ = Client

1A Ⓓ Kevin Creative Ⓒ Eclipse Creative 1B Ⓓ Carmi e Ubertis Milano Srl 1C Ⓓ Fossil Ⓒ Zodiac

2A Ⓓ GingerBee Creative Ⓒ Eagle Transit 2B Ⓓ Nynas Ⓒ Tucker Music Works 2C Ⓓ Truly Design Ⓒ Truly Design

3A Ⓓ Steele Design Ⓒ Eastman Outdoors 3B Ⓓ Schwartzrock Graphic Arts Ⓒ Wiese Creative 3C Ⓓ tomvasquez.com Ⓒ newsweek

4A Ⓓ Paragon Marketing Communications Ⓒ Kuwait Oil Company 4B Ⓓ Mojo Solo Ⓒ Falcon Labs 4C Ⓓ lunabrand design group Ⓒ Legacy Sports

A

B

C

1

2

3

4

D = Design Firm   **C** = Client

1A **D** Rickabaugh Graphics **C** Bowling Green State University   1B **D** Extra Point Creative **C** unused   1C **D** Spiral Design Studio **C** Quick & Reilly

2A **D** 7981design **C** yadagroup   2B **D** Church Art Works **C** Soar   2C **D** BPG Design **C** Al Mal Capital

3A **D** Office For Design **C** Boudouris   3B **D** Hubbell Design Works   3C **D** orton design **C** falcon express international

4A **D** Design Invasion **C** American Steel Fabrication   4B **D** Jerron Ames **C** Arteis   4C **D** BRANDSTORM CREATIVE GROUP **C** Latin Cargo Airlines

A

B

C

1

Metropolitan
National Bank

2

Eastbourne
EAGLES

SOUTHERN MISS

3

4

D = Design Firm **C** = Client

1A **D** Karl Design Vienna **C** Delikatessen / Dortmunder Brauerei 1B **D** Ray Dugas Design **C** Hawkeye Industries 1C **D** Studio GT&P **C** Cantina Fratelli Pardi
2A **D** Design Matters Inc! 2B **D** Rickabaugh Graphics **C** University of Louisiana, Monroe 2C **D** Traction **C** Florence Freedom Baseball Team
3A **D** Eagle Imagery **C** Eastbourne Eagles 3B **D** Scott Oeschger **C** Saint Joseph's Preparatory School 3C **D** RARE Design **C** University of Southern Mississippi
4A **D** Rickabaugh Graphics **C** Marquette University 4B **D** Stacy Bormett Design, LLC **C** Flacons athletic department 4C **D** Turnstyle **C** Seattle University

1

2

3

XTO
whistler
2006

EAGLE
BOARDS
by FANATIC

4

D = Design Firm   **C** = Client

1A **D** Sayles Graphic Design, Inc. **C** Microware   1B **D** Colin Saito **C** Gearhawk   1C **D** Artrinsic Design **C** Hillgrove High School—Powder Springs, GA

2A **D** Studio Simon **C** Lancaster JetHawks   2B **D** Karl Design Vienna **C** Adler Apotheke Dachsbach   2C **D** davpunk! **C** SteelHawk Airsoft

3A **D** McQuillen Creative Group **C** Northstar District Sioux Council   3B **D** Squires and Company **C** XTO Energy   3C **D** Karl Design Vienna **C** Fanatic Windsurfing

4A **D** Church Art Works **C** Diocese of Arlington   4B **D** Hotiron Creative, LLC **C** Phoenix Marketing   4C **D** Kitemath **C** Rumble Pigeons

A **B** **C**

PHOENIX
GRAND
HOTEL

1

NASWA
TEMPE 08 ARIZONA

2

3

COFFEE
Darling

SILVER PHOENIX

PHOENIX™

4

D = Design Firm **C** = Client

1A **D** Glitschka Studios **C** BAM Agency **1B** **D** Type G **C** Desert Phoenix **1C** **D** Mission Creative **C** Phoenix Fitness
2A **D** Glitschka Studios **C** BAM Agency **2B** **D** Velocity Design Group **C** NASWA **2C** **D** Glitschka Studios **C** BAM Agency
3A **D** DesignLingo **C** Nature Society Symbol **3B** **D** Thinking*Room, Inc. **C** Ven Hin **3C** **D** Ginter & Miletina
4A **D** Hoyne Design **C** Cafe Racer **4B** **D** Entropy Brands **C** Silver Phoenix, LLC **4C** **D** PositiveZero, Ltd. **C** PHOENIX

A   **B**   **C**

1

Aguila De Oro
PRODUCTIONS

2

phoenix

F E N I X

3

Phoenix

PMG
WEALTH MANAGEMENT

PHOENIX
AUDIOVISUAL

4

GRANDPRIX
ARIZONA™

PHOINIX
ENTERPRISES

PHOENICIAN
FUNDRAISING

D = Design Firm   **C** = Client

1A **D** Friends University **C** Ark Church   1B **D** Thelogoloft.com   1C **D** Greteman Group **C** Greteman Group

2A **D** Glitschka Studios **C** BAM Agency   2B **D** Tactix Creative **C** The City of Phoenix, Arizona   2C **D** DesignLingo **C** Fenix Night Club

3A **D** Riham AlGhussein   3B **D** Ten26 Design Group, Inc. **C** PMG Wealth Managment   3C **D** Robert Price **C** Advantage Business Communications

4A **D** Campbell Fisher Design **C** Champ Car   4B **D** Tandem Design Agency **C** Phoinix Enterprises   4C **D** Effusion Creative Solutions

A **B** **C**

1

2

3

4

ⅅ = Design Firm   **ℂ = Client**

1A ⅅ Sound Mind Media ℂ Aaron Price   1B ⅅ Diagram   1C ⅅ Webster Design Associates, Inc. ℂ Phoenix Partnership

2A ⅅ Tandem Design Agency ℂ Wilson Kester Law   2B ⅅ Burocratik - Design ℂ Adriano Esteves   2C ⅅ Murillo Design, Inc. ℂ KGB Texas

3A ⅅ Hubbell Design Works ℂ The Port of Long Beach   3B ⅅ ZupiDesign ℂ Pletz   3C ⅅ Struck ℂ Calle Soccer

4A ⅅ Moker Ontwerp ℂ Dos Palomas Negras   4B ⅅ Blake BW ℂ Pigeon Productions   4C ⅅ Black Osprey Dead Arts ℂ MAGIC BULLET RECORD

A **B** **C**

1

PEACE

2

3

4

Ⓓ = Design Firm   Ⓒ = Client

1A Ⓓ Judson Design Ⓒ Judson Design **1B** Ⓓ Imaginaria Ⓒ World Faith **1C** Ⓓ Fernandez Design Ⓒ EGL, Eagle Global Logistics

2A Ⓓ Strange Ideas **2B** Ⓓ Geneva Marketing Group Ⓒ Interfaith Volunteer Caregivers of Fayette INC. **2C** Ⓓ Richard Bloom Studio Ⓒ Chabad

3A Ⓓ Sabingrafik, Inc. Ⓒ Charlotte Russe **3B** Ⓓ TrueBlue, Inc. Ⓒ DRS Marketing **3C** Ⓓ ArtGraphics.ru Ⓒ Kvartira.ru Investment Corporation

4A Ⓓ Church Logo Gallery **4B** Ⓓ Fernandez Design Ⓒ EGL, Eagle Global Logistics **4C** Ⓓ Howerton+White Ⓒ College Hill United Methodist

A

B

C

PEACEFUL & PROUD
Personalized Care for Veterans

1

PROVENA
Health

Banco Libertad Bank SSB

2

London Abused
Women's Centre

3

Tiempo
de Vida

4

D = Design Firm　**C** = Client

1A **D** Kari Piippo Oy　**C** Mikkelin seurakunta　1B **D** Draplin Design Co.　**C** RE:VOLVE Apparel Project　1C **D** robin ott design　**C** Hospice of the Western Reserve

2A **D** Monigle Associates, Inc.　**C** Provena Health　2B **D** angryporcupine*design　**C** David Bennett Consulting　2C **D** The Netmen Corp　**C** Libertad Bank

3A **D** Blue Storm Design　**C** Medical Matters　3B **D** McGuire Design　**C** Christ Lutheran Church　3C **D** Honey Design　**C** London Abused Women's Centre

4A **D** Adams Design Group　**C** Fantail Property Services　4B **D** Creative Impact, Inc.　**C** Esperanza Cadena　4C **D** Greteman Group

1

2

3

4

D = Design Firm   **C** = Client

1A **D** Black Crow Studio **C** Catholic Diocese of Sacramento   1B **D** Church Logo Gallery   1C **D** Ray Dugas Design **C** human rights watch
2A **D** Greteman Group   2B **D** Eggra **C** Piazza   2C **D** Rule29 **C** Life in Abundance
3A **D** Felixsockwell.com **C** NCAYV, USA   3B **D** Mary Hutchison Design, LLC **C** TisBest, LLC   3C **D** Miriello Grafico, Inc. **C** Age Concerns
4A **D** Grey Matter Group **C** Bella Vista Church   4B **D** BenKandoraDESIGN **C** White Birds   4C **D** hecht design **C** Transition House

A **B** **C**

1

2

3

4

ⅅ = Design Firm **ⓒ** = Client

1A ⅅ Bryan Cooper Design ⓒ Hope Education 1B ⅅ Glitschka Studios ⓒ BarkingPhish.com 1C ⅅ KENNETH DISENO ⓒ Hope for the future lectures, by J. L. Gonzalez

2A ⅅ David & Associates ⓒ Cargill Incorporated 2B ⅅ Wages Design ⓒ Peachtree Corners Presbyterian Church 2C ⅅ Catalyst Logo Design ⓒ Hospice of Central Virginia

3A ⅅ Union Design & Photo ⓒ Peace and Plenty Fine Antiques 3B ⅅ Sabingrafik, Inc. ⓒ Old Creek Ranch 3C ⅅ Sabingrafik, Inc. ⓒ Old Creek Ranch

4A ⅅ VanPaul Design ⓒ nashero 4B ⅅ Pink Tank Creative ⓒ Voiceless Watch 4C ⅅ Daniel Sim Design

A **B** **C**

1

2

3

4

D = Design Firm **C** = Client

1A **D** Felixsockwell.com **1B** **D** Page Design **C** Impax World **1C** **D** Strange Ideas

2A **D** Schwartzrock Graphic Arts **C** Westwood Lutheran Church **2B** **D** Dustin Commer **C** Emily Weiss **2C** **D** Diagram **C** Human Rights Watch

3A **D** Dogstar **C** Benjamin Middaugh **3B** **D** Helix Design Communications **C** Conceptual **3C** **D** LeBoYe **C** Lippo Group

4A **D** Dennard, Lacey & Associates **C** First Assembly of God **4B** **D** Ray Dugas Design **C** Human Rights **4C** **D** Thielen Designs **C** Hyperactive Music Magazine

A

B

C

VINCERE
GOLF & SPORT

1

CRIBBS
CAUSEWAY

BAD SCHWALBACH

DataWing
SOFTWARE

2

SUSTAINABLE
REDWOOD CITY

PEDDADA.
conspicuously progressive™

JANELLE

3

zoopack

jazz
by Mobilink

4

ⓓ = Design Firm **ⓒ = Client**

A   **B**   **C**

1

2

3

4

Ⓓ = Design Firm   Ⓒ = Client

1A Ⓓ Straka-Design Ⓒ Birdyard Pet Shop   1B Ⓓ Banowetz + Company, Inc. Ⓒ Criterion Development Partners   1C Ⓓ Van Vechten Creative Ⓒ Just For Girlfriends

2A Ⓓ e-alw.com Ⓒ Student's Travel, Poland   2B Ⓓ Banowetz + Company, Inc. Ⓒ Criterion Development Partners   2C Ⓓ Glitschka Studios

3A Ⓓ Phinney Bischoff Design House Ⓒ Sawtooth Lodge   3B Ⓓ Esparza Advertising Ⓒ The Retreat at Corrales Overlook

3C Ⓓ Insight Design Ⓒ Healthy Bird Brand Products

4A Ⓓ Werner Design Werks Ⓒ Indochine   4B Ⓓ Sabingrafik, Inc. Ⓒ Oliver McMillin   4C Ⓓ Graphic-FX Ⓒ First Baptist Concord

A

B

C

1

2

COMO PARK
ZOO & CONSERVATORY

3

4

ⓓ = Design Firm   ⓒ = Client

1A ⓓ Hutchinson Associates, Inc. ⓒ Cardinal 1B ⓓ Hutchinson Associates, Inc. ⓒ Cardinal 1C ⓓ DUSTIN PARKER ARTS ⓒ Curt Clonts
2A ⓓ Glitschka Studios ⓒ Bird Fellow 2B ⓓ DUEL Purpose ⓒ Dirt Poor Robins 2C ⓓ Home Grown Logos ⓒ River Rat Poker Wear
3A ⓓ Fernandez Design ⓒ Newland Communities 3B ⓓ Fernandez Design ⓒ Newland Communities
3C ⓓ Yamamoto Moss Mackenzie ⓒ Como Park Zoo & Conservatory
4A ⓓ NOMADESIGN Inc. ⓒ OOISI 4B ⓓ Howling Good Designs ⓒ Dick Amper 4C ⓓ Opolis Design, LLC ⓒ Greener Pastures Poultry

A **B** **C**

1

JCB
El futuro de su marca

mailbox
tees

Briar Chapel

2

3

4

(blue) - adj.

D = Design Firm   **C** = Client

1A D Sol Consultores **C** JCB **1B D** arin fishkin **C** Mailbox Tees **1C D** Fernandez Design **C** Briar Chapel **2A D** Jon Flaming Design **C** Arrington Oil & Gas
2B D Sabingrafik, Inc. **C** Morrow Development **2C D** ginger griffin marketing and design **C** Sandy Tilley **3A D** Stiles Design **C** Tequila Mockingbird
3B D Gary Sample Design **C** Highland's High School (Kentucky) **3C D** UlrichPinciotti Design Group **C** Toledo Mud Hens Baseball Club
4A D Glitschka Studios **C** Smartacus **4B D** Mohouse Design Co. **C** Up & Away, Inc. **4C D** Carrihan Creative Group **C** Arcane Tees

A   B   C

1

2

3

4

D = Design Firm   **C** = Client

1A **D** Extraverage Productions   **C** Personal   **1B** **D** Oxide Design Co.   **C** Meadowlark Recycling   **1C** **D** Sibley Peteet   **C** El Pato Mexican Restaurants

2A **D** The Netmen Corp   **C** Little Chicken   **2B** **D** United States of the Art   **C** Station zwei   **2C** **D** Hula+Hula   **C** Ibero 909

3A **D** Double Brand   **C** Fiu   **3B** **D** Finch Creative   **C** Finch Creative   **3C** **D** Denis Olenik Design Studio   **C** ZooSmart

4A **D** Denis Olenik Design Studio   **C** ZooSmart   **4B** **D** edesign   **C** The Primary Day School   **4C** **D** United States of the Art

A **B** **C**

1

2

3

4

D = Design Firm **C** = Client

1A **D** TFI Envision, Inc. **C** United Methodist Homes 1B **D** Howling Good Designs **C** Brady & Honaski Associates
1C **D** Atlantis Visual Graphics **C** Birds of a Feather Birdseed 2A **D** Clockwork Studios **C** Austin Crows Football Club
2B **D** The Modern Brand Company **C** Canterbury Cabinetry 2C **D** PUSH Branding and Design **C** Condor Enterprises of Iowa
3A **D** yellow dog design **C** CROW Antiques, LLC 3B **D** Paradox Box 3C **D** Gyula Nemeth **C** Vertigo Studio
4A **D** Tower of Babel **C** Rook's Nook Cafe 4B **D** Christian Rothenhagen **C** Berlin Native Clothing 4C **D** Diagram

A

B

C

1

2

3

4

D = Design Firm   C = Client

1A **D** Burn Creative **C** Laing Group   1B **D** Hinge **C** World Bank   1C **D** Kahn Design **C** Positive Purpose, Inc.

2A **D** Simple Creative Design **C** Christina Erlach Sevaistre   2B **D** orangebird **C** Orange Bird Creative   2C **D** Think Cap Design **C** Fancy Works

3A **D** Maremar Graphic Design **C** Lillia Molina   3B **D** Funnel:Eric Kass:Utilitarian+Commercial+Fine·Art **C** Saarinen   3C **D** Glitschka Studios **C** Bird Fellow

4A **D** Rickabaugh Graphics **C** University of Texas at San Antonio   4B **D** Fredrik Lewander **C** Swedish Salman Rushdie Committee

4C **D** VIVA Creative Group **C** Tembloroso Tshirt Company

A

B

C

1

2

3

4

D = Design Firm   **C** = Client

1A **D** Judson Design **C** Tambi Martin   **1B** **D** KTD **C** OWL Displays   **1C** **D** Tomko Design **C** Land and See

2A **D** High Fiber Design **C** Terrace Hill Golf Club   **2B** **D** FDTdesign **C** City of Asuni, Italy   **2C** **D** www.yifenglin.com **C** Juice Jill

3A **D** HendrixRaderWise **C** HRW   **3B** **D** Ray Dugas Design **C** Owl Bay Publishing   **3C** **D** Nectar Graphics **C** Atticus Wine

4A **D** Grow Design **C** Sakonnet Wisewatch   **4B** **D** Little Jacket **C** Bohemian Foundation   **4C** **D** *tabula rasa* graphic design **C** Bentley College

A

B

C

1

2

3

4

D = Design Firm **C** = Client

1A **D** Extra Point Creative **C** unused 1B **D** Rickabaugh Graphics **C** Florida Atlantic University 1C **D** Gable Design Group **C** Wild Animal Clinic Foundation

2A **D** Deep Design **C** The HoneyBaked Ham Company 2B **D** Graphismo **C** The Haviland Family 2C **D** L*U*K*E **C** Jake O'Connor's Public House

3A **D** Steven O'Connor **C** Cruz/Kravetz:ideas for El Pollo Loco 3B **D** Jennifer Braham Design **C** Reliable Organics 3C **D** Noble **C** Tyson

4A **D** Decoylab **C** Early Jewelry 4B **D** Trapdoor Studio **C** Mary~Maxine 4C **D** Trapdoor Studio **C** Rooster Productions

1

2

3

4

D = Design Firm   **C** = Client

1A D Brand Anarchy Group   **C** Clavo Music   **1B D** Dino Design   **C** PB Bell Homes   **1C D** Red Olive Design   **C** Tartar

2A D Nectar Graphics   **C** Pudding River Cellars   **2B D** Banowetz + Company, Inc.   **C** Criterion Development Partners   **2C D** Oxide Design Co.   **C** Boss Studios

3A D A3 Design   **C** mattamy homes   **3B D** Bryan Cooper Design   **C** Poultry Litter Solutions   **3C D** Ivey McCoig Creative Partners   **C** Southern Fidelity Mortgage

4A D R&R Partners   **4B D** NeoGrafica   **C** DELJI Poultry   **4C D** Honest Bros.   **C** Rise & Shine Media

A

B

C

1

2

3

4

D = Design Firm   **C** = Client

1A **D** Karl Design Vienna **C** Deutz-Fahr Landmaschinen   1B **D** Hammerquist & Nebeker **C** Red Torpedo   1C **D** Red Circle **C** RipIFX Group
2A **D** Hinge **C** The Wing Fanatic Sports Theatre & Grill   2B **D** Advertising Ventures, Inc.   2C **D** Pikant marketing **C** Regional health organisation
3A **D** Landor Associates **C** Pathe   3B **D** Juicebox Designs **C** Urban Hen   3C **D** The Know **C** Chook
4A **D** Studio Simon **C** Toledo Mud Hens   4B **D** cincodemayo **C** Ollie's Fried Chicken   4C **D** Advertising Ventures, Inc.

A
B
C

1

COCKTAILS

california chicken cafe

ROOSTER
BLEND

2

3

SUNRISE
PICTURES

MINORITY
ROOSTER

Gallo
CERVEZA

4

BIG
COCK
RACING

ⓓ = Design Firm   ⓒ = Client

1A ⓓ Gridwerk ⓒ Cocktails Bar & Restaurant **1B** ⓓ ARTini BAR ⓒ CCC **1C** ⓓ Bryan Cooper Design ⓒ Dark Shades, Inc.

2A ⓓ Pikant marketing ⓒ Regional health organisation **2B** ⓓ Gardner Design ⓒ Willow Creek Designs **2C** ⓓ Salty Design Foundry ⓒ Farm Chicks

3A ⓓ co:lab ⓒ Sunrise Pictures **3B** ⓓ Extra Point Creative ⓒ unused **3C** ⓓ ADC Global Creativity ⓒ Gallo Cerveza

4A ⓓ Opolis Design, LLC ⓒ Greener Pastures Poultry **4B** ⓓ the design spring ⓒ BCR Team **4C** ⓓ Oscar Morris ⓒ Rodriguez Salsa

1

2

3

4

D = Design Firm   **C** = Client

1A **D** Steven O'Connor **C** JD Inc.   1B **D** Rufuturu **C** STROGANOVA STUDIO   1C **D** Go Welsh   2A **D** Sabingrafik, Inc.   **C** Quail Ridge

2B **D** Richards Brock Miller Mitchell & Associates   **C** Golden State Movers   2C **D** Barnstorm Creative Group Inc   **C** Burrard International

3A **D** Pure Brand Communications   **C** Riot Golf   3B **D** DesignPoint, Inc.   **C** Treo Ranches   3C **D** Designland   **C** slow roasted duck website development

4A **D** Publicis   4B **D** Miller Meiers Design for Communication   **C** Dan Rood Design   4C **D** Red Olive Design   **C** Distaff

A
B
C

1

2

3

4

D = Design Firm **C** = Client

1A D brandStrata **C** Disney **1B D** The Logo Factory, Inc. **C** Duck Surfboards **1C D** Fresh Oil **C** America's Choice Products

2A D 2TREES DESIGN **C** MarZ Hot Rods **2B D** Hornall Anderson **C** Pacific Coast Feather **2C D** Hornall Anderson **C** Quackers Clothiers

3A D Emerge Design Group **C** Match Play Enterprises **3B D** A3 Design **C** mattamy homes **3C D** Jerron Ames **C** Arteis

4A D Cappelli Communication srl **C** Dukapis Ltd **4B D** Gary Sample Design **C** Great Lakes Developers **4C D** Paragon Marketing Communications **C** Al Bahar Center

A **B** **C**

1

2

3

4

D = Design Firm **C** = Client

1A **D** Koester Design **C** Tramell Crow 1B **D** Kingston Partners **C** Swan Development Advisors 1C **D** David Kampa **C** Shoreline Grill
2A **D** Tactix Creative **C** Paul Howalt 2B **D** Funk/Levis & Associates, Inc. **C** South Pointe 2C **D** Strategy Studio **C** Starret
3A **D** Funnel:Eric Kass:Utilitarian+Commercial+Fine:Art **C** Central Indiana Land Trust 3B **D** GingerBee Creative **C** Blue Heron Art Glass
3C **D** Brand Engine **C** Cost Plus World Market 4A **D** Eagle Imagery **C** Little Stork Baby Boxes 4B **D** Extra Point Creative **C** unused
4C **D** hecht design **C** Kingfisher

A   **B**   **C**

1

SAN FRANCISCO BAY
BIRD OBSERVATORY

TERN CAPITAL

BlueCargo

2

mailrx

3

PEÑASCO

RESORTS

4

SOLD!

Paradocks
EAST COAST GRILLE

ToucanSmoothies

D = Design Firm   **C** = Client

1A D Alterpop **C** San Francisco Bay Bird Observatory   **1B D** Daniel Scharfman Design, Inc. **C** Tern Capital, LLC
1C D DAGSVERK—Design and Advertising **C** Bluebird Cargo
2A D Guernsey Graphics **C** Kiwi Press   **2B D** Burton (Snowboards) Corp. **C** Burton Snowboards   **2C D** Cocoon **C** Mail Rx
3A D Tactix Creative **C** Riptide   **3B D** Doink, Inc. **C** Miami Benefit Club   **3C D** Prejean Creative **C** Backroads & Bayous
4A D Spork Design, Inc. **C** Tom Parrott   **4B D** Pure Fusion Media **C** Paradocks   **4C D** Jeff Ames Creative **C** Toucan International

A

B

C

1

2

3

4

ⓓ = Design Firm   ⓒ = Client

1A ⓓ yantra design group, inc ⓒ Quetzal Designs International   1B ⓓ TFI Envision, Inc. ⓒ Romora Bay Club   1C ⓓ Qualitá Design ⓒ Prefeitura Municipal de Guaratuba

2A ⓓ Sayles Graphic Design, Inc. ⓒ Microware   2B ⓓ Denis Olenik Design Studio ⓒ ZooSmart   2C ⓓ Ginter & Miletina ⓒ Walkabout

3A ⓓ Rumfang ⓒ Nordic Institute of Asian Studies   3B ⓓ mooci design labs ⓒ South Asian International Film Festival   3C ⓓ Gardner Design ⓒ ClearNeon

4A ⓓ Art Passions Design ⓒ Art Passions Design   4B ⓓ Culture Pilot ⓒ Evoke Photography   4C ⓓ Bryan Cooper Design ⓒ Fair Isaac, Inc.

A   **B**   **C**

1

EL PINQUINO
REDONDO BEACH, CA

2

ARI
ASSOCIATE REFRIGERATION INC.

3

4

D = Design Firm   **C** = Client

1A **D** Carmi e Ubertis Milano Srl   **C** Frisco   1B **D** mugur mihai   **C** Gideon Cardozo Communications   1C **D** Judson Design   **C** yacht owner

2A **D** Arena Design   **C** ARI   2B **D** Keyword Design   **C** Benjamin's Refrigeration   2C **D** Kindred Design Studio, Inc.   **C** Ice Breakers Online Dating Service

3A **D** 9MYLES, Inc.   **C** Advanced Coating systems   3B **D** Glitschka Studios   **C** Advanced Refrigeration & Air   3C **D** Big Communications

4A **D** Little Jacket   **C** Tony Margherita Management / Wilco   4B **D** Blue Tomato Graphics   **C** Red Penguin Mobile Marketing   4C **D** logobyte   **C** Aspen Sno

A

B

C

1

2

3

4

ⓓ = Design Firm ⓒ = Client

1A ⓓ Luke Baker ⓒ Rainfall Media **1B** ⓓ FREEHALL. Diseño & Ilustración ⓒ FAR **1C** ⓓ Weylon Smith **2A** ⓓ Sabingrafik, Inc. ⓒ Canyon Hills
2B ⓓ Sabingrafik, Inc. ⓒ Seafarer Baking Company **2C** ⓓ EMC illustration & design ⓒ Siesa, LLC **3A** ⓓ Gardner Design
3B ⓓ Art Craft Printers & Design ⓒ Feather Your Nest Home Furnishings Boutique **3C** ⓓ Banowetz + Company, Inc. ⓒ East Dallas Developmental Center
4A ⓓ NeonBeige ⓒ Stork, Custom Baby Planning **4B** ⓓ asmallpercent ⓒ Nest **4C** ⓓ Theory Associates ⓒ Zaytoon Mediterranean Wraps

A **B** **C**

1

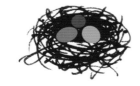

NestEggPapers

2

3

4

D = Design Firm **C** = Client

1A **D** TOKY Branding+Design **C** David Eichholtz **1B** **D** Nectar Graphics **C** Willow Nest **1C** **D** Banowetz + Company, Inc. **C** Nest Egg Papers

2A **D** Element **C** Nvest Wealth Strategies **2B** **D** Elumin Creative Agency **C** The IRA Store **2C** **D** ANS **C** FeatherKraft Kayaks

3A **D** Clore Concepts **C** Spirit Savvy Business **3B** **D** Karl Design Vienna **C** BBS **3C** **D** The Martin Group **C** Ad Pro Sports

4A **D** Dotzero Design **C** Davis Agency **4B** **D** Jerron Ames **C** Arteis **4C** **D** Design Hovie Studios, Inc. **C** Hawk Solutions

A

B

C

1

2

3

4

D = Design Firm   **C** = Client

1A **D** Karl Design Vienna **C** FCB / Debitel AG   **1B** **D** e-alw.com **C** Kolinstal, Poland   **1C** **D** pictogram studio **C** SwiftWing

2A **D** Ross Levitt **C** IDS—ID Society   **2B** **D** Miles Design **C** Premier Sports Chiropractic   **2C** **D** 7981design **C** ILE Textiles

3A **D** Anoroc **C** Trousdale School   **3B** **D** Hornall Anderson **C** Eos   **3C** **D** RARE Design **C** University of Southern Mississippi

4A **D** Sabingrafik, Inc. **C** Marabou   **4B** **D** rainy day designs **C** The Birdbrain   **4C** **D** Hirshorn Zuckerman Design Group **C** 7 Nations Lacrosse Co.

A　**B**　**C**

1

2

3

4

D = Design Firm　**C** = Client

1A D Casscles Design, Inc **C** Soccer United Marketing　**1B D** Art Craft Printers & Design　**C** Feather Your Nest Home Furnishings Boutique
1C D Open Creative Group **C** Visu Artists　**2A D** Ulyanov Denis **C** Ypsilon　**2B D** S&N Design **C** Four & Twenty Blackbirds
2C D Art Craft Printers & Design **C** Feather Your Nest Home Furnishings Boutique
3A D Zwoelf Sonnen **C** City of Bad Schwalbach　**3B D** pearpod **C** bevy management　**3C D** Advertising Intelligence
4A D Schwartzrock Graphic Arts **C** BI　**4B D** futska llc **C** rubbish gallery　**4C D** Christian Rothenhagen **C** dlxsf skateboardshop

A

B

C  **1**

 **2**

 **3**

 **4**

D = Design Firm   **C** = Client

1A **D** McGarrah/Jessee **C** Costa Del Mar   1B **D** Marc Posch Design, Inc **C** Jurgen & Lorenz Strasser   1C **D** Sabingrafik, Inc. **C** Chaos Lures

2A **D** Dogstar **C** SanRoc Cay   2B **D** The Netmen Corp   2C **D** themarsdesign.net **C** Anthony's Fish Grotto   3A **D** David Russell Design **C** Chip Latimer

3B **D** Hubbell Design Works **C** The Adventure Center   3C **D** Marlin   4A **D** United States of the Art

4B **D** Braue: Brand Design Experts **C** Judel Vrolijk & Co. Design & Engineering GmbH   4C **D** Chermayeff & Geismar, Inc. **C** Sailfish Point

A

B

C

1

2

3

4

D = Design Firm   **C = Client**

1A **D** Glitschka Studios **C** Pirana Systems   1B **D** Device   1C **D** Dotzero Design **C** Tanner Accounting

2A **D** Ray Dugas Design **C** Lake's Catfish Farm   2B **D** RARE Design **C** Temple Baptist Church   2C **D** Torch Creative **C** FIN

3A **D** Owen Design **C** Bluefish   3B **D** Fernandez Design **C** Catch My Drift   3C **D** Bryan Cooper Design **C** Tulsa Zoo

4A **D** Barnstorm Creative Group, Inc **C** Piscine Energetics   4B **D** Storm Corporate Design Ltd. **C** New Zealand Outfitters   4C **D** Tip Top Creative **C** Princess Tours

A

B

C

1

2

3

SCREAMING FI
INSTORM·IMPLEMENT·EXEC

4

Ⓓ = Design Firm   Ⓒ = Client

1A Ⓓ Qualità Design Ⓒ Fishin Pescados   1B Ⓓ CRE8 design co. Ⓒ West Central Telephone Association   1C Ⓓ Toledo Area Metroparks Ⓒ Metroparks of the Toledo Area

2A Ⓓ Saltree Pty Ltd Ⓒ Coles Myer / Label House   2B Ⓓ Fresh Oil Ⓒ Tou Bagaille Beach Bar Restaurant   2C Ⓓ Enforme Interactive Ⓒ Moore Wealth Incorporated

3A Ⓓ Sellier Design, Inc. Ⓒ Screaming Fish   3B Ⓓ Hubbell Design Works Ⓒ blufish, LLC   3C Ⓓ Just2Creative Ⓒ Proposed

4A Ⓓ Howling Good Designs Ⓒ The Bay Place, Long Island's Classroom by the Sea   4B Ⓓ Sabingrafik, Inc. Ⓒ Birch Aquarium   4C Ⓓ Sabingrafik, Inc. Ⓒ Tamarindo Diria

A

B

C

1

2

3

4

D = Design Firm   **C** = Client

1A **D** Bryan Cooper Design **C** OHFS   1B **D** Extra Point Creative **C** Hirschmann Design **C** Foothills League

2A **D** Keyword Design **C** Highland Downtown Association Community Mural Project   2B **D** The Martin Group **C** Big Fish Property Management Services

2C **D** Artnak **C** Artnak   3A **D** Glitschka Studios **C** Samurai Guppy Tropical Fish   3B **D** Your Eyes Here **C** Kristi Coy Real Estate   3C **D** futska llc **C** futska

4A **D** Sussner Design Company **C** Reflections   4B **D** CRE8 design co. **C** Reel Addiction Charters   4C **D** HendrixRaderWise **C** Odyssey Group

A B C

1

2

3

4

D = Design Firm **C** = Client

1A **D** Paradox Box **C** «Barracuda» 1B **D** Cirque de Darmon **C** self 1C **D** The Image Designers Group **C** Key West Fish Company
2A **D** Velocity Design Group **C** self promotion 2B **D** The Netmen Corp 2C **D** The Logo Factory, Inc.
3A **D** Sabingrafik, Inc. **C** Crazy Shirts 3B **D** Todd M. LeMieux Design **C** Ludlow Fish Market 3C **D** DUEL Purpose **C** Roadside Cinema
4A **D** Windup Design **C** Anderson Bait Company 4B **D** David Maloney **C** Walton's Wildlife 4C **D** Compass Design **C** Bucking Bass Brewing Company

A **B** **C**

1

2

3

4

D = Design Firm   **C** = Client

1A **D** Studio Simon **C** Toledo Walleye   1B **D** Richards Brock Miller Mitchell & Associates **C** Cow Creek Ranch   1C **D** Dotzero Design **C** Dotzero
2A **D** Sabingrafik, Inc. **C** Rustic Ventures   2B **D** The Martin Group **C** WTS   2C **D** Moss Creative **C** Houston's Restaurants
3A **D** Entropy Brands **C** Territory Anglers   3B **D** Tactix Creative **C** Fishfood.net   3C **D** RARE Design **C** 589 Family Fish House
4A **D** Visual Inventor Ltd. Co. **C** Hogan/TMK   4B **D** Giles Design, Inc. **C** The Sandbar Fish House & Market   4C **D** CD Austin **C** Snapper Jacks

A

BLACK'S
BAR AND KITCHEN

B

LIGHTBOURNE
HOUSE

C

TRUE NORTH
FEDERAL CREDIT UNION

1

Naughtyfish

XTO 2008
Caymans

2

STRAY CAT
DESIGN GROUP

3

Naked FISH
RESTAURANT

RumbleFish
NEWS·READER

FISH
FRY

4

D = Design Firm   **C** = Client

1A **D** Shelter Studios **C** Black Restaurant Group   1B **D** Galperin Design, Inc. **C** Lightbourne House Estate   1C **D** Phinney Bischoff Design House **C** True North

2A **D** TRUF **C** Mamash Restaurant   2B **D** Naughtyfish **C** Naughtyfish Design   2C **D** Squires and Company **C** XTO Energy

3A **D** LSD **C** edivinmarket store   3B **D** Jerron Ames **C** Arteis   3C **D** Iskender Asanaliev **C** Iskender Asanaliev

4A **D** ZAYASDESIGN **C** Naked Fish Restaurant   4B **D** The Logo Factory, Inc.   4C **D** Hutchinson Associates, Inc. **C** St. Josaphat School

A **B** **C**

1

2

3

4

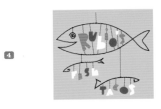

D = Design Firm   **C** = Client

1A **D** Dogstar **C** Sea Science Center 1B **D** Sabingrafik, Inc. **C** University of California, San Diego 1C **D** 7th Street Design **C** Natsume Koi Farm

2A **D** Ray Dugas Design **C** Ray Dugas Design 2B **D** Blue Clover **C** Waterside 2C **D** Blue Sky Design, Inc. **C** Pacífico Restaurant

3A **D** Hubbell Design Works **C** Passionfish 3B **D** *tabula rasa* graphic design **C** Cambridge Arts Council 3C **D** Squires and Company **C** XTO Energy

4A **D** Sabingrafik, Inc. **C** Rubios Baja Grill 4B **D** Whaley Design, Ltd **C** Krewe de Walleye, MN Cajun & Zydeco, Music and Dance Association

4C **D** Campbell Fisher Design **C** Malee's

FISH, BUGS, REPTILES

A
B
C

1

CAYMANS
XTO 2008

Fluga & net

BAHAMIAN FUSION
the cuisine of Cotton Bay

2

Rubio's Baja Grill

Rubio's
BAJA GRILL

3

redphish

BIGKAHUNA!
R E C O R D S

4

D = Design Firm   C = Client

1A **D** Schwartzrock Graphic Arts **C** Target   1B **D** Sabingrafik, Inc. **C** Rubios Baja Grill   1C **D** Sabingrafik, Inc. **C** Rubios Baja Grill
2A **D** Squires and Company **C** XTO Energy   2B **D** O! **C** Fluga & net   2C **D** Helium Creative, Inc. **C** Cotton Bay Estates & Villas
3A **D** Sabingrafik, Inc. **C** Rubios Baja Grill   3B **D** Sabingrafik, Inc. **C** Rubios Baja Grill   3C **D** Richard Underberg **C** Scorching Fish
4A **D** Heck Yeah! **C** Technologic   4B **D** Glitschka Studios **C** Green Living Magazine   4C **D** John Silver **C** Big Kahuna! Records

A

B

C

1

SistersCare

2

BROMAN○DELL
TACKLE DESIGN

swell
fish and chips

NordWest
FischumschlagsZentrale

3

EcoSeafood
Naturally the World's Finest Seafood

Punto Náutico

4

Voyage

LittleFish
Patent Investement
& Protection Group

D = Design Firm   **C** = Client

1A **D** Hubbell Design Works **C** Leighton Hubbell   1B **D** Nick Glenn Design **C** Sisters Care; Christian Care Center   1C **D** Karl Design Vienna **C** Braue / Q-Bioanalytic

2A **D** Fredrik Lewander **C** Johan Broman   2B **D** Back2Front **C** Paul Ankertell   2C **D** Braue: Brand Design Experts **C** NordWest GmbH

3A **D** A3 Design   3B **D** Axiom Design Partners **C** Eco Seafood   3C **D** Juancazu **C** punto náutico

4A **D** 7981design **C** Veken Real Estate   4B **D** Kastelov **C** Voyage   4C **D** NOMADESIGN Inc. **C** LttleFish

A	**B**	**C**	
			**1**
			**2**
			**3**
			**4**

D = Design Firm   **C** = Client

1A **D** Incitrio **C** bigfish consulting   1B **D** Gizwiz Studio **C** Hooked Up   1C **D** David Kampa **C** H.E.B. Foodstores

2A **D** Sabingrafik, Inc. **C** The Masters Group   2B **D** Hep **C** Superfresh   2C **D** Sabingrafik, Inc. **C** Cranford Group

3A **D** Judson Design **C** Continental Airlines   3B **D** Jenn David Design **C** Pisces Studio   3C **D** Judson Design **C** Bill Meek

4A **D** HMK Archive **C** TG&O   4B **D** Judson Design **C** Cushman Wakefield   4C **D** Ink Graphix **C** Nacksving Studio

A   **B**   **C**

1       

2   

3    

4       

D = Design Firm   **C** = Client

1A **D** Brand Engine   **C** Cost Plus World Market   1B **D** mad studios   **C** JIUU group of creatives   1C **D** HMK Archive   **C** Lynnette Embrey

2A **D** noe design   **C** Shedd Aquarium   2B **D** KENNETH DISENO   **C** Sistemas acuicolas intensivos   2C **D** Dustin Commer   **C** Indian Hills

3A **D** Garfinkel Design   **C** Trinity Gear   3B **D** Glitschka Studios   **C** QuickSilver   3C **D** Tunglid Advertising Agency ehf.   **C** Snæfellsbær

4A **D** Hubbell Design Works   **C** Certi-Fresh Seafood Company   4B **D** Ion Design, Inc.   **C** Coral Gardens

4C **D** THE GENERAL DESIGN CO.   **C** National Coalition for Marine Fisheries

 **A**

 **B**

 **C** **1**

 **2**

 **3**

 **4**

D = Design Firm **C** = Client

1A **D** Tactix Creative **C** Liar's Corner 1B **D** Naughtyfish **C** Naughtyfish Design 1C **D** Nectar Graphics **C** A Benefit for Yamhill County Food Bank

2A **D** BlaseDesign **C** Mamasake Sushi Restaurant 2B **D** Lee Davis Design **C** Tyfish Systems 2C **D** Judson Design **C** Olympia Grill

3A **D** Artnak **C** Ivancic 3B **D** Sabingrafik, Inc. **C** Crazy Shirts 3C **D** ORFIK DESIGN **C** Municipality of Rethymno

4A **D** 7981design **C** Hangzhou Polar Ocean Park 4B **D** Kevin Creative **C** MissionMedia 4C **D** Sabingrafik, Inc. **C** Simple Green

1

2

3

4

D = Design Firm   **C** = Client

1A **D** Velocity Design Group **C** self promotion   1B **D** Delikatessen **C** REWE Supermarkets   1C **D** Delikatessen **C** REWE Supermarkets

2A **D** BrandBerry **C** Plastic whale   2B **D** Bryan Cooper Design **C** Orbit   2C **D** Victor Goloubinov **C** NefteGasMach

3A **D** Remo Strada Design **C** Whale Communications   3B **D** Diagram   3C **D** Mad Dog Graphx **C** Bowhead

4A **D** Art Chantry **C** Washington State Department of Tourism   4B **D** Sabingrafik, Inc. **C** S. D. Johnson Company   4C **D** Green Bird Media **C** Hammer Real Estate

A

B

C

1

2

3

4

D = Design Firm **C** = Client

1A **D** Richards Brock Miller Mitchell & Associates **C** Hammerhead 1B **D** fuszion **C** Baltimore Aquarium

1C **D** Clockwork Studios **C** Youth Basketball League of Salt Lake City 2A **D** Cuie&Co **C** White Shark Adventures 2B **D** Popgun **C** Tommy's Baseball Team

2C **D** Tactix Creative **C** Chaparral High School 3A **D** Eagle Imagery **C** Central Park Football Club, Singapore

3B **D** About350, Inc. **C** Busch Entertainment Corporation 3C **D** Hyperakt **C** Circle Line Downtown

4A **D** Rickabaugh Graphics **C** University of South Carolina Beaufort 4B **D** Farm Design **C** Swimming Team 4C **D** Clockwork Studios **C** Sixman Football Association

A   **B**   **C**

1

2

3

4

D = Design Firm   **C** = Client

1A **D** Robot Creative **C** Law Offices of Charles E. Zech   1B **D** Velocity Design Group **C** Expressions   1C **D** Gizwiz Studio **C** Sharks Southbury

2A **D** Karl Design Vienna **C** Starfish Restaurant   2B **D** Cacao Design **C** Aqua Sail   2C **D** Lunar Cow **C** Shark XX

3A **D** TFI Envision, Inc. **C** Maritime Aquarium at Norwalk   3B **D** Visible Ink Design **C** Richard East Productions   3C **D** Sire Advertising **C** Selinsgrove Area School District

4A **D** Honey Design **C** The City of London   4B **D** The Robin Shepherd Group **C** FLUID Surfboards   4C **D** Courtney & Company **C** The Ritz-Carlton, Grand Cayman

A

DEEP SEA FLYING

B

C HOTEL SEYCHELLES
BEACH ESTATE · ANGUILLA

1

OCEAN DAWN
LUXURY WATERFRONT SUITES

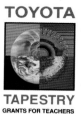

TOYOTA
TAPESTRY
GRANTS FOR TEACHERS

DENVER MUSEUM OF NATURE & SCIENCE

2

pearline

PADRE ISLAND
NATIONAL SEASHORE

INTERMOCC
Monitoring and Control

3

Sparks
POOL RESTAURANT

suavesabores

Boatgal

4

D = Design Firm   **C** = Client

1A **D** O'Hare Design **C** Crazy Shirts 1B **D** Gardner Design **C** Somnograph 1C **D** mugur mihai **C** Gideon Cardozo Communications
2A **D** Hexanine **C** Ocean Dawn 2B **D** Pinnacle Design Center **C** Toyota & National Science Teachers' Association
2C **D** Monigle Associates Inc. **C** Denver Museum of Nature & Science 3A **D** Diagram 3B **D** Boelts Design **C** Western National Parks Association
3C **D** FutureBrand **C** Intermocc 4A **D** Go Graphic **C** Jiyeh Marina Resort 4B **D** Sebastiany Branding & Design **C** Ondina
4C **D** Flying Chicken Studios **C** Boater's Life

A **B** **C**

1

Southwest Radiation Oncology

2

CRAB CAY
EXUMA, BAHAMAS

3

LAGNIAPPE
FOOD COURT

4

MARISCO
Islamar

CAFE CREOLE
RESTAURANT

ⅅ = Design Firm **ⓒ = Client**

1A ⒹRoskelly Inc. ⒸIsland Time Clothing 1B ⒹBryan Cooper Design ⒸOHFS 1C ⒹThe Office of Marc Bostian ⒸSouthwest Radiation Oncology
2A ⒹJudson Design ⒸCushman Wakefield 2B ⒹSabingrafik, Inc. ⒸCranford Group 2C ⒹZwoelf Sonnen ⒸSebastian Krebs
3A ⒹLisa Brussell Design ⒸCaché Foods LLC 3B ⒹPrejean Creative ⒸPeninsula Gaming 3C ⒹPrejean Creative ⒸBackroads & Bayous
4A ⒹKW43 BRANDDESIGN ⒸKuhlmann Beauty 4B ⒹBurocratik - Design ⒸFricar 4C ⒹCreative Madhouse ⒸCafe Creole Restaurant

1

2

3

4

D = Design Firm   **C** = Client

1A **D** Glitschka Studios **C** Upper Deck Company   1B **D** reaves design **C** octo   1C **D** Judson Design **C** Olympia Grill

2A **D** KNOCK, inc. **C** KNOCK, inc.   2B **D** Judson Design **C** Olympia Grill   2C **D** Zwoelf Sonnen **C** self

3A **D** Salty Design Foundry **C** Let's Dive   3B **D** Combustion **C** End To End   3C **D** Zwoelf Sonnen **C** self

4A **D** Thielen Designs **C** Tevi Schwartz   4B **D** Roskelly Inc. **C** Octopus Software   4C **D** eindruck design

A   **B**   **C**

1

OCEANIA

BLUE

DAHL
FLIESEN—NATURSTEIN

2

TURKS & CAICOS

3

KAILIA

SAVANNAH RIVER
PRESERVE
— SOUTH CAROLINA —

CAYMAN
ISLANDS

4

PODillow

PETTINGA

D = Design Firm   **C** = Client

1A **D** XY ARTS **C** Oceania   1B **D** morrow mckenzie design   1C **D** Zwoelf Sonnen

2A **D** Karl Design Vienna **C** Riverboat Classics   2B **D** Sabingrafik, Inc. **C** Chileno Bay   2C **D** Think Cap Design **C** Turks & Caicos

3A **D** this is nido **C** kailia shoes   3B **D** RIGGS **C** The Nature Conservancy of SC   3C **D** Sabingrafik, Inc. **C** The Masters Group

4A **D** Nynas **C** Turtle Cove Neighborhood Association   4B **D** LogoMotto.com **C** PODillow / Brent Doud   4C **D** Semisans **C** Mark Pettinga, Financial Advisor

 A

 B

 C

1

2

3

4

D = Design Firm   **C** = Client

1A **D** gocreativ   1B **D** The Robin Shepherd Group   **C** Jacksonville Film Festival   1C **D** Daggerfin   **C** AlixPartners

2A **D** Narita Design   **C** Praia do Forte Eco Resort   2B **D** Squires and Company   **C** XTO Energy   2C **D** concussion, llc   **C** Fort Worth Zoo

3A **D** The BrandingHouse   **C** The Littlest Golfer, Inc.   3B **D** WISE Graphic Design   **C** Julie Tam   3C **D** Christine Case Design   **C** Roger Williams Park Zoo

4A **D** Cirque de Darmon   **C** self   4B **D** Kineto   **C** Hilton Cebu Phillipines   4C **D** Glitschka Studios   **C** Upper Deck Company

A **B** **C**

1

2

3

4

ⅅ = Design Firm **ⅽ = Client**

1A ⅅ Glitschka Studios ⅽ Harry Potter 1B ⅅ Glitschka Studios ⅽ The Marketing Store Worldwide 1C ⅅ Whitney Edwards, LLC ⅽ BAI Aerosystems

2A ⅅ Glitschka Studios ⅽ NFL License 2B ⅅ Rickabaugh Graphics ⅽ Florida A&M University 2C ⅅ Sabingrafik, Inc. ⅽ Consolite Corporation

3A ⅅ Home Grown Logos ⅽ Average To Elite 3B ⅅ Eric Medalle Design ⅽ Snakes on a Plate Softball Team 3C ⅅ 343 Creative ⅽ AFL

4A ⅅ Stiles Design ⅽ King Snake 4B ⅅ brandStrata ⅽ Eve Elliott 4C ⅅ Alphabet Arm Design ⅽ Static of the Gods

A  B  C

   1

Mexican Cultural Center
of Northern California

2

3

4

D = Design Firm   **C** = Client

1A **D** Campbell Fisher Design **C** Arizona Rattlers   1B **D** Union Design & Photo **C** Snake Snare   1C **D** 7981design **C** yuandingFurniture

2A **D** Black Crow Studio **C** Mexican Cultural Center of Northern California   2B **D** Tactix Creative **C** Clin One   2C **D** Red Olive Design **C** Hibernaculum

3A **D** scott adams design associates **C** adam cards   3B **D** Dotzero Design **C** Kritis   3C **D** Cooper Design **C** PythonLab

4A **D** Chris Malven Design **C** Essencia   4B **D** The Laster Group **C** GECU   4C **D** Strange Ideas

A

B

C

1

2

3

OLDSKOOL

4

D = Design Firm   **C** = Client

1A **D** Atomic Wash Design Studio **C** Cobra Metal Works, Inc   1B **D** CDI Studios **C** Viper Industries   1C **D** MSI **C** Golfsmith

2A **D** MSI **C** Golfsmith   2B **D** Esparza Advertising **C** New Mexico Animal Cruelty Task Force   2C **D** MSI **C** Golfsmith

3A **D** DTM_INC **C** HomeBrew Records   3B **D** Extra Point Creative   3C **D** Extra Point Creative

4A **D** Alphabet Arm Design **C** Tyrannosaurus Records   4B **D** Charles Akins_AkinsTudio **C** Bank South   4C **D** Studio Simon **C** East Texas Pump Jacks

1

2

3

4

ⓓ = Design Firm　　**ⓒ = Client**

1A ⓓ Daniel Sim Design ⓒ DinoHaven　1B ⓓ Topo ⓒ X world police & fire games　1C ⓓ Kraftaverk - Design Studio

2A ⓓ CAPSULE ⓒ Gatorback　2B ⓓ Studio Tandem ⓒ Gator Cad　2C ⓓ Webster Design Associates, Inc. ⓒ Crocs Bar & Grill

3A ⓓ Webster Design Associates, Inc. ⓒ Crocs Bar & Grill　3B ⓓ Barnstorm Creative Group, Inc ⓒ Florida Everblades Hockey

3C ⓓ Jolly Dog, Ltd ⓒ Chuck Ross/Tampa Bay Blues Fest　4A ⓓ O'Hare Design ⓒ Fraze Pavilion　4B ⓓ Storm Design, Inc. ⓒ Gator's Towing

4C ⓓ Gary Sample Design ⓒ Wally Pop

A

B

C

1

2

3

4

D = Design Firm **C = Client**

1A **D** Helius Creative Advertising **C** Desert Canyons Development 1B **D** Patlejch **C** Swinging Pictures 1C **D** Brand Engine **C** Cost Plus World Market

2A **D** Velocity Design Group **C** Cravings Restaurant 2B **D** Gary Sample Design **C** Philosophics, Inc. 2C **D** Velocity Design Group **C** Cravings Restaurant

3A **D** Courtney & Company **C** The Ritz-Carlton, Grand Cayman 3B **D** Double Brand **C** Latin Club 3C **D** Gary Sample Design **C** Philosophics, Inc.

4A **D** Gizwiz Studio **C** Adam Ferenzii 4B **D** Ray Dugas Design **C** Cooking Light Magazine 4C **D** Boelts Design **C** Arts Festival

A

B

C

1

2

3

4

ⅅ = Design Firm   ⅭＣ = Client

1A ⅅ Traction Ⅽ Maggy's Sports Grill 1B ⅅ reaves design Ⅽ calypso lizard 1C ⅅ Dragyn Studios Ⅽ Haapiti Surf Lodge

2A ⅅ Schwartzrock Graphic Arts Ⅽ Design Center, Inc. 2B ⅅ Gábor Lakatos Ⅽ Gábor Lakatos 2C ⅅ Colorblind Chameleon Ⅽ Colorblind Chameleon

3A ⅅ renaud garnier smart rebranding Ⅽ Kiss that frog 3B ⅅ Ziga Aljaz Ⅽ City 3C ⅅ Jacq Design, LLC Ⅽ bigMOXY.com

4A ⅅ HuebnerPetersen Ⅽ Salome High School 4B ⅅ D&Dre Creative Ⅽ Little Leapers Daycare 4C ⅅ wray ward Ⅽ sir eds

A　　　**B**　　　**C**

1

2

3

4

D = Design Firm　**C** = Client

1A **D** Schuster Design Group **C** Eventa　1B **D** Stream Creative **C** Frogneck Web Solutions　1C **D** Daniel Sim Design

2A **D** The Logo Factory, Inc.　2B **D** Diagram　2C **D** vladimir sijerkovic **C** Ulu Lana

3A **D** Device　3B **D** LogoMotto.com **C** CellFrog.com　3C **D** Blue Tricycle, Inc. **C** Dancing Toad, Inc.

4A **D** logobyte **C** Web Frogger　4B **D** innfusion studios **C** HotPad　4C **D** PureMatter Brand Marketing + Interactive **C** American Advertising Federation

A

B

C

1

2

3

4

D = Design Firm   **C** = Client

1A **D** Black Barn Brand Design **C** Leaps & Bounds Pediactric Therapy   1B **D** Judson Design **C** Leap Network   1C **D** Diagram

2A **D** noe design   2B **D** noe design **C** Sara Hillebrand   2C **D** Redonk Marketing **C** The Lily Pad

3A **D** The Netmen Corp   3B **D** The Logo Factory, Inc. **C** The Frog Pond   3C **D** Culp Design **C** The Happy Frog Copy Center

4A **D** Schwartzrock Graphic Arts **C** Freshwater Community Church   4B **D** Rhombus, Inc. **C** Rowley Enterprises   4C **D** Via Grafik **C** bstrkt industries

A   **B**   **C**

1

2

3

4

D = Design Firm   **C** = Client

1A **D** concussion, llc **C** Fort Worth Zoo   1B **D** Made on Earth **C** Made on Earth   1C **D** Toledo Area Metroparks **C** Metroparks of the Toledo Area

2A **D** Strange Ideas   2B **D** Burocratik - Design **C** Selketface   2C **D** The Image Group **C** National Nail Corp.

3A **D** Raymond Creative Group **C** Morehouse School of Medicine   3B **D** Sabingrafik, Inc. **C** Cranford Group   3C **D** Device

4A **D** Always Creative **C** Spider Spray   4B **D** Artnak **C** Mental picture   4C **D** Miles Design **C** Jeanette Lee

1

2

3

4

D = Design Firm **C** = Client

1A **D** designheavy **C** Webuilders 1B **D** BarkinSpider Studio **C** Seth Meierotto, BarkinSpider Studio 1C **D** Tactix Creative

2A **D** String **C** Premium/ PSC 2B **D** joni dunbar design **C** Mitchell Pest Control 2C **D** Scribblers' Club **C** The Bug Rug

3A **D** Diagram 3B **D** Altagraf **C** Bee Positive 3C **D** Jobi **C** Jobi

4A **D** The Netmen Corp 4B **D** The Flores Shop **C** Little Techie 4C **D** Jerron Ames **C** Arteis

A
 B
 C

1

2

3

4

D = Design Firm   **C** = Client

1A **D** paralleldesigned **C** ZEFER & Flyswat   1B **D** Karl Design Vienna **C** Spirit / Superfly Radio   1C **D** Glitschka Studios **C** Upper Deck Company

2A **D** Glitschka Studios **C** Templin Brink Design   2B **D** www.mieland.de **C** Mephisto   2C **D** Glitschka Studios **C** Templin Brink Design

3A **D** Karl Design Vienna **C** Spirit / Superfly Radio   3B **D** POLLARDdesign **C** FireFly Creative   3C **D** Banowetz + Company, Inc. **C** Hotel ZaZa

4A **D** Opolis Design, LLC **C** Firefly   4B **D** Opolis Design, LLC **C** Firefly   4C **D** The Logo Factory, Inc.

	A	B	C
1			
2			
3			
4			

D = Design Firm **C** = Client

1A **D** Grey Matter Group **C** Firefly Life 1B **D** Ross Hogin Design **C** Stacy and Angie 1C **D** twentystar **C** Firefly Digital Media

2A **D** Rhombus, Inc. **C** Jobe Watersports 2B **D** BrandExtract **C** Glow Labs 2C **D** LeBoYe **C** Graha Realty Kencana

3A **D** Eli Atkins Design **C** Life, Love, Ladybugs 3B **D** Stream Creative **C** Four Seasons Town Centre 3C **D** UNO **C** Lady Bug

4A **D** Brian Blankenship **C** Cuddly Bugs 4B **D** Fernandez Design **C** Briar Chapel 4C **D** Glitschka Studios **C** Loui Loui Sportswear

A

B

C

1

2

3

4

D = Design Firm   **C** = Client

1A **D** WONGDOODY **C** Hip Cricket   1B **D** RedBrand **C** Saltamontes   1C **D** Zwoelf Sonnen **C** Peter Kohl

2A **D** Pepper Group **C** Life Fitness   2B **D** Zwoelf Sonnen **C** Chitin Cuisine   2C **D** reaves design **C** ant farm consulting

3A **D** Aranzamendez Design and Productions **C** Shalom Baby   3B **D** Sabingrafik, Inc. **C** Mires Design   3C **D** Brian Krezel **C** Marmot Outdoor

4A **D** Home Grown Logos **C** Tawnya Archer   4B **D** Robot Creative **C** Back House Bead Company   4C **D** Spoonbend **C** Art of Wigs

 A

 B

 C

1

2

3

4

ⅅ = Design Firm   **ⓒ = Client**

1A ⅅ Riley Designs   1B ⅅ Sayles Graphic Design, Inc.   ⓒ Busy Bee Tailoring   1C ⅅ Sauvage Design   ⓒ Worker Bees

2A ⅅ Carrihan Creative Group   ⓒ TracFone   2B ⅅ Visual Moxie   ⓒ Killer Bees Art   2C ⅅ Cisneros Design   ⓒ Bumble Bee's Baja Grill

3A ⅅ Mystic Design, Inc.   ⓒ Buzz Thru Joe's   3B ⅅ Boelts Design   ⓒ TCI Summer Buzz Icon   3C ⅅ Element   ⓒ element

4A ⅅ David Kampa   ⓒ Laurie Darlin Brewing Company   4B ⅅ Chanpion Design   ⓒ Bumbl Pty Ltd   4C ⅅ Kradel Design   ⓒ Beehive Thrift Store

	A	B	C
1			
2			
3			
4			

D = Design Firm   C = Client

1A **D** Hirschmann Design **C** Vanderhoof Elementary School   1B **D** 01d **C** Cleaning Bees   1C **D** Just2Creative **C** The Miami Herald

2A **D** The Robin Shepherd Group **C** Beeline, Inc.   2B **D** Carrihan Creative Group **C** TracFone   2C **D** Thirtythr33

3A **D** canvas design consultants **C** Baby Bumble Bee Australia   3B **D** Alphabet Arm Design **C** Dave Balter / BzzAgent, LLC

3C **D** Paradox Box **C** City administration, Beeline   4A **D** Home Grown Logos **C** Azz & Bzz Apparel

4B **D** Hayes+Company **C** Wellington County Brewery, Inc.   4C **D** Karmalaundry **C** Radialbee

 **A**

 **B**

 **C** **1**

 **A**

 **B**

 **C** **2**

 **A**

 **B**

 **C** **3**

 **A**

 **B**

 **C** **4**

D = Design Firm   **C** = Client

1A **D** Daniel Sim Design **C** Hollywood Bee   1B **D** Jerron Ames **C** Arteis   1C **D** Chris Rooney Illustration/Design **C** Beatrice and Benedick

2A **D** Brandient **C** Apidava SRL   2B **D** Nynas **C** HoneyBee   2C **D** Hubbell Design Works **C** Nectar Industrial

3A **D** Schwartzrock Graphic Arts **C** Ascent Marketing   3B **D** Blue Bee Design **C** Blue Bee Design   3C **D** Savage-Olsen Design Engineering, Inc.

4A **D** reaves design **C** DDB   4B **D** Strange Ideas   4C **D** Stiles Design **C** Vespaio Restaurant

A

B

C

1

2

3

4

D = Design Firm   **C** = Client

1A **D** Glitschka Studios **C** Bzzy Bee Insurance 1B **D** Glitschka Studios **C** Bzzy Bee Insurance 1C **D** Hirshorn Zuckerman Design Group **C** InPhonex

2A **D** Axiom **C** Antenna Records 2B **D** Prolific **C** Los Alamos reading program 2C **D** Kastelov **C** Librasia

3A **D** Gabi Toth **C** Adobe Systems Romania 3B **D** Ivan Manolov **C** Top Print 3C **D** Sakkal Design

4A **D** Keyword Design **C** Dunes Learning Center 4B **D** The Robin Shepherd Group **C** St. Johns Realty Group 4C **D** LSD **C** un mundo feliz / a happy world production

1

2

3

4

D = Design Firm   **C** = Client

1A **D** Mindgruve **C** ClubLife   1B **D** Spark Studio **C** Evergreen Retirement Finance   1C **D** Go Media **C** Nature League

2A **D** Graphic D-Signs, Inc. **C** LandscaperMarketing.com   2B **D** Ad Impact Advertising **C** Worldwide Online Printing   2C **D** R&R Partners **C** Nathan Adelson Hospice

3A **D** DEMOLID Inc. **C** Egis   3B **D** Built Creative **C** House of Hope, Shelter for Young Women   3C **D** D&Dre Creative **C** Ana Brasil

4A **D** Moscato Design **C** Sarah & Ira Winner   4B **D** IE Design + Communications **C** Moth Vintage Couture   4C **D** Gardner Design **C** Lavish Boutique

A

EMBRYO

B

Herbacious

C

CHOOSE YOUR CAUSE

1

belle & baz
LONDON

2

podcastready

vaada

3

virtutech

Nelly

4

meghan B.

Catalyst
center of
aesthetic medicine
& wellness

D = Design Firm   **C** = Client

1A **D** Embryo Design 1B **D** Culture A.D. **C** Urban Bazaar 1C **D** TRUF **C** BabaKul Jewelry

2A **D** Kane and Associates **C** Belle & Baz 2B **D** Nien Studios **C** Beckstrand Cancer Foundation 2C **D** ars graphica **C** podcastready

3A **D** Spark Studio **C** Victorian Alcohol and Drug Association 3B **D** Hornall Anderson **C** Virtutech 3C **D** Daniel Sim Design **C** Biogreen Consulting

4A **D** Straka-Design **C** Sat.1 4B **D** Tricia Hamon/Pear Tree Design **C** Meghan Biesiadecki 4C **D** Sundog **C** Catalyst

A   **B**   **C**

  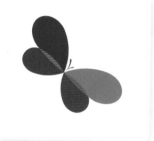

1

2

Catalyst
equity group

Sweet Beginnings

lojas
viva™

3

sollievo
BE HOME. LIVE LIFE.

nourish LLC
Feed the Body. Free the Mind.

Jardins de Sant'Iago
CONDOMINIO FECHADO

4

D = Design Firm   **C** = Client

1A **D** Gardner Design **C** Lavish   1B **D** Logoholik **C** Tao Living   1C **D** El Paso, Galeria de Comunicacion **C** Asociacion Turistica Valle de Benasque

2A **D** eight a.m. brand design (shanghai) Co., Ltd **C** yuanxinld makeup   2B **D** ellen bruss design **C** Monarch   2C **D** Gardner Design **C** Lavish Boutique

3A **D** Gardner Design **C** Catalyst   3B **D** Ondine Design **C** St. Francis Medical Center   3C **D** Burocratik - Design **C** Lojas Viva

4A **D** Miles Design **C** Alzheimers Care Group   4B **D** Clockwork Studios **C** Nourish   4C **D** I'm Design **C** ImopaixÃ£o

A

B

C

1

2

3

4

D = Design Firm   **C** = Client

1A **D** Mattson Creative   1B **D** Mindgruve   **C** ClubLife   1C **D** Jason Pillon   **C** Maya Pillon

2A **D** Jason Pillon   **C** Choice for Children Education Foundation   2B **D** Pennebaker   **C** FKP Architects   2C **D** WONGDOODY   **C** Good First Nutritionals

3A **D** Pink Tank Creative   **C** Transplant Australia   3B **D** Porkka & Kuutsa Oy   **C** Clairia Oy   3C **D** Lippincott   **C** SK Group

4A **D** Gardner Design   **C** Hullings Orthodontics   4B **D** Gardner Design   **C** Lavish Boutique   4C **D** Gardner Design   **C** Lavish

A

B

C

1

2

3

4

D = Design Firm   **C** = Client

1A **D** Meg Levine Design **C** Imanima   1B **D** Ulyanov Denis **C** Elinor   1C **D** Kevin Creative **C** Insight Developments

2A **D** Pat Taylor, Inc. **C** Beautiful Printers, Inc.   2B **D** ars graphica **C** Blue Valentine   2C **D** Sebastiany Branding & Design **C** Flor de Botao

3A **D** True Perception **C** Plastic Surgeon   3B **D** Sayles Graphic Design, Inc. **C** McArthur Company   3C **D** Sibley Peteet **C** Sanders\Wingo

4A **D** Culture Pilot **C** theorie   4B **D** Ray Dugas Design **C** Hope Homes   4C **D** Bradshaw Design **C** T. Zoraz

A　　　**B**　　　**C**

1

2

3

4

D = Design Firm　**C** = Client

1A **D** Bertz Design Group **C** Nurtur　1B **D** Shawn Huff **C** Brooklyn Huff　1C **D** Howling Good Designs **C** Jodi Richards

2A **D** Gardner Design **C** Lavish　2B **D** Miller Creative, LLC **C** Papillon Lingerie　2C **D** vladimir sijerkovic **C** Shmitten

3A **D** Gardner Design **C** Lavish Boutique　3B **D** Thelogoloft.com **C** Dynamic Change　3C **D** Gardner Design **C** Catalyst

4A **D** Gardner Design **C** Child Behavior Specialists　4B **D** Tribe Design, LLC　4C **D** markatos | moore **C** Swallowtail Home Furnishings

A

B

C

1

2

3

4

D = Design Firm   **C** = Client

1A **D** Jeff Kern Design **C** Project Rescue—Robison Creative Studios   1B **D** Heisel Design **C** Mary's on Bayshore   1C **D** Gateway Communications

2A **D** Bradshaw Design **C** Kodak   2B **D** Grafikona, design studio **C** BairMesocare Cosmetics   2C **D** The Netmen Corp

3A **D** the medium **C** The Nursery   3B **D** Robot Creative **C** ASNA   3C **D** The Action Designer **C** Norsk Ideutvikling

4A **D** Gardner Design **C** ClearNeon   4B **D** Karl Design Vienna **C** R. Schuch, Austria   4C **D** Sommese Design **C** Lauth Development

A

B

C

1

2

for every woman

NEW MEXICO
Cosmetic Lasering

3

Thanksgiving in April

Francijas pavasaris
UN PRINTEMPS FRANÇAIS
LATVIJA 07 LETTONIE

4

Grace

International Adoption Agency

D = Design Firm   **C** = Client

1A **D** Gardner Design **C** Plastic Surgery Center   1B **D** Viziom **C** Vzanz Waxing Center   1C **D** J.Williams Design **C** Gerber

2A **D** Jeff Kern Design **C** Assemblies of God   2B **D** Dotzero Design **C** CHAO   2C **D** Squires and Company **C** New Mexico Cosmetic Lasering

3A **D** R&R Partners **C** Catholic Charities   3B **D** APSITS **C** France Culture Ministry   3C **D** R&R Partners **C** Nathan Adelson Hospice

4A **D** More Branding+Communication **C** Avondale Cottage   4B **D** Tchopshop Media **C** Grace International Adoption Agency   4C **D** Ditto! **C** Butterfly Tales

A

B

C

1

2

3

4

D = Design Firm   **C** = Client

1A **D** Kjetil Vatne **C** Mongrel Records 1B **D** Clockwork Studios **C** Sixman Football Association 1C **D** POLLARDdesign **C** DeMarini

2A **D** Rickabaugh Graphics **C** Louisiana Tech 2B **D** Schwartzrock Graphic Arts **C** Design Center 2C **D** Tactical Magic **C** Union University

3A **D** R&R Partners 3B **D** Studio Simon **C** Golden Baseball League 3C **D** Rickabaugh Graphics **C** University of Connecticut

4A **D** JumpDog Studio **C** Auburn University 4B **D** Graphismo **C** Georgetown Animal Shelter 4C **D** Leah Hartley **C** Mad Dog Productions

A **B** **C**

1

2

3

4

D = Design Firm   C = Client

1A **D** Sibley Peteet **C** Buddy Systems   1B **D** Turner Duckworth **C** Method   1C **D** Fernandez Design **C** Circuit City

2A **D** Greteman Group **C** Kansas Humane Society   2B **D** Stiles Design **C** Black Lab Advertising   2C **D** Fernandez Design **C** Circuit City

3 A **D** McArtor Design   3B **D** Fernandez Design **C** Circuit City   3C **D** Gyula Nemeth **C** Dirty Dogs

4A **D** Judson Design **C** Tickle + Blagg Animal Hospital   4B **D** Sauvage Design **C** Physiotherapets   4C **D** Felixsockwell.com **C** none—for sale

1

2

3

4

Ⓓ = Design Firm   Ⓒ = Client

1A Ⓓ Fernandez Design Ⓒ Circuit City   1B Ⓓ Kastelov Ⓒ Royal Canine   1C Ⓓ Brandient Ⓒ Dedeman

2A Ⓓ Modus Design, Inc. Ⓒ Dash   2B Ⓓ Killustration, Ink. Ⓒ Dogrrific.com   2C Ⓓ Delikatessen Ⓒ HTS GmBH

3A Ⓓ Indicia Design Inc Ⓒ Spinnaker Web Design   3B Ⓓ Richards Brock Miller Mitchell & Associates Ⓒ F45   3C Ⓓ Leah Hartley Ⓒ Mad Dog Productions

4A Ⓓ graphic granola Ⓒ Bark for Peace!   4B Ⓓ ginger griffin marketing and design Ⓒ Dos Mundos de Santa Fe   4C Ⓓ Vincent Burkhead Studio Ⓒ Canine Genius

A

B

C

1

2

3

4

D = Design Firm   **C** = Client

1A **D** The Bradford Lawton Design Group **C** Just Fur Me   1B **D** Langton Cherubino Group **C** Lani's Line, LLC   1C **D** CF Napa Brand Design **C** Stevenot Winery

2A **D** Leah Hartley **C** SASI Marketing/Farmdog.com.au   2B **D** Karl Design Vienna **C** ARAS Tiernahrung   2C **D** The Logo Factory, Inc. **C** Big Bark, Inc.

3A **D** Sabingrafik, Inc. **C** Project Nate   3B **D** Sabingrafik, Inc. **C** Project Nate   3C **D** Rickabaugh Graphics **C** Black Dog Lacrosse

4A **D** Carrihan Creative Group **C** Bishop Hendricken High School   4B **D** c moto **C** Big Bone Beer   4C **D** Banowetz + Company, Inc. **C** Frenkel & Frenkel

A

B

C

1

2

3

4

D = Design Firm **C** = Client

1A **D** Jolly Dog, Ltd **C** Jolly Dog 1B **D** The Logo Factory, Inc. 1C **D** Martin Branding Worldwide **C** Convenience Foods

2A **D** GCG **C** Rahr Beer 2B **D** Dustin Commer **C** Kansas Humane Society 2C **D** James Olson Design **C** Duluth Trading

3A **D** Reactive Mediums **C** Bay Blue Kennels 3B **D** Kitemath **C** The Barker Shop 3C **D** Tactix Creative **C** Subzero Design

4A **D** Alphabet Arm Design **C** Mud Dog Media Company 4B **D** The Robin Shepherd Group **C** LOC DOGGZ

4C **D** The Joe Bosack Graphic Design Co. **C** Youngstown Steelhounds

| | **A** | **B** | **C** |

1

2

3

4

D = Design Firm   **C** = Client

1A **D** Sabingrafik, Inc. **C** Harcourt & Co.   **1B** **D** Sayles Graphic Design, Inc. **C** Kirke Financial Services   **1C** **D** The Logo Factory, Inc. **C** Scraps Dog Bakery

2A **D** Moss Creative **C** Black+White, LLC   **2B** **D** Gary Sample Design **C** Bad Dawg   **2C** **D** Janet Allinger **C** Stephanie Schriver

3A **D** Sayles Graphic Design, Inc. **C** Big Dog Screen Printing   **3B** **D** Insight Design **C** Big Dog Motorcycles, Inc.   **3C** **D** Fumiko Noon **C** Fritzy's

4A **D** Green Dog Studio **C** Houndstooth Bakery   **4B** **D** Mazemedia   **4C** **D** Sussner Design Company **C** saint barts

A

B

C

1

2

3

4

D = Design Firm **C** = Client

1A D Jeff Fisher LogoMotives **C** Black Dog Furniture Design **1B D** Hubbell Design Works **C** Purina Dog Chow **1C D** Advertising Intelligence

2A D Blue Studios, Inc. **C** ScorePatrol **2B D** mccoycreative **C** Sherpa Dog **2C D** Rickabaugh Graphics **C** Wilson & Associates

3A D Marc Posch Design, Inc **C** Justin Rudd **3B D** DUSTIN PARKER ARTS **C** Blue Dog Bakery **3C D** Marc Posch Design, Inc **C** Justin Rudd

4A D Sussner Design Company **C** pardon my french bakery **4B D** Dirty Design **C** Nouveau Filth **4C D** Type G **C** DogStar

A B C

1

2

3

4

ⓓ = Design Firm ⓒ = Client

1A ⓓ Fuelhaus Brand Strategy + Design ⓒ Spotya Quickcash 1B ⓓ retropup ⓒ Paper Dog Design 1C ⓓ Leah Hartley ⓒ Mad Dog Productions

2A ⓓ Jerron Ames ⓒ Arteis 2B ⓓ Dustin Commer ⓒ Mark Warren 2C ⓓ Bryan Cooper Design ⓒ Dog Park

3A ⓓ graphic granola ⓒ Bark For Peace! 3B ⓓ Bryan Cooper Design ⓒ Paws and Claws 3C ⓓ RedBrand ⓒ Datik

4A ⓓ graphic granola ⓒ Raising Canine 4B ⓓ Northfound ⓒ Catering St. Louis 4C ⓓ Home Grown Logos ⓒ Doggy D Tails

A

B

C

 **1**

 **2**

 3

 4

Ⓓ = Design Firm   **Ⓒ = Client**

1A Ⓓ The Netmen Corp Ⓒ Dog beds and more   1B Ⓓ Bulldog & Braun   1C Ⓓ Brandient Ⓒ Loyalia
2A Ⓓ Jennifer Braham Design Ⓒ Camp 4 Paws   2B Ⓓ Sabingrafik, Inc. Ⓒ Zonk, Inc.   2C Ⓓ Advertising Intelligence
3A Ⓓ Houston & Ⓒ Blind Dog Studio   3B Ⓓ Houston & Ⓒ Blind Dog Studio   3C Ⓓ Houston & Ⓒ Blind Dog Studio
4A Ⓓ Totem Ⓒ YouGetItBack.com   4B Ⓓ Ross Hogin Design Ⓒ Bad Dog Sportswear   4C Ⓓ Howerton+White Ⓒ dogsgone.org

1

the bone yard

2

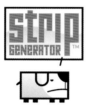

3

4

D = Design Firm   **C** = Client

1A **D** Stiles Design   **C** Humane Society   **1B** **D** Totem   **C** YouGetItBack.com   **1C** **D** SVP Partners   **C** The Bone Yard
2A **D** Ziga Aljaz   **C** Strip Generator   **2B** **D** 01d   **C** 4legs   **2C** **D** reaves design
3A **D** Roskelly Inc.   **C** The Potter League for Animals   **3B** **D** Fernandez Design   **C** Tracy Locke   **3C** **D** Fernandez Design   **C** Citrix
4A **D** STUBBORN SIDEBURN   **C** Stubborn Sideburn   **4B** **D** STUBBORN SIDEBURN   **C** hipposchemes   **4C** **D** Modern Dog Design Co.   **C** Olive Dog Products

A

B

C

1

2

3

4

D = Design Firm   **C** = Client

1A **D** Thinking Cap Design **C** Alaska Jack   1B **D** Greteman Group   1C **D** Sabingrafik, Inc. **C** Teen Center Café

2A **D** Sabin Design **C** Foster Farms   2B **D** Sabin Design **C** Foster Farms   2C **D** Hubbell Design Works **C** Leighton Hubbell

3A **D** Glitschka Studios **C** Publisher   3B **D** Fossil **C** Fossil   3C **D** Elevation Creative Studios **C** Quando

4A **D** Jonathan Rice & Company **C** Red Lab   4B **D** Fresh Oil **C** Shaggy Chic Pet Boutique   4C **D** Design Outpost **C** UrbanOutsitters

A **B** **C**

1

2

3

4

D = Design Firm **C** = Client

1A **D** Glitschka Studios **C** Color Lab 1B **D** Liquid Inc **C** ID Watchdog 1C **D** Quentin Duncan **C** nextbigthing.co.za

2A **D** Lunar Cow **C** Humane Society of Greater Akron 2B **D** Steven O'Connor **C** Meyers Kennel Club 2C **D** Hip Street **C** Down River Dogs Eatery

3A **D** Rickabaugh Graphics **C** Texas A&M University 3B **D** Rickabaugh Graphics **C** University of Connecticut

3C **D** Rickabaugh Graphics **C** University of South Dakota 4A **D** Carol Gravelle Graphic Design **C** Wheele, Inc.

4B **D** Gizwiz Studio **C** Doggy Danish 4C **D** A3 Design **C** Mattamy Homes

A   B   C

KLONDIKE

1

FOXY DOG

lead boy

GoodDogArt
BY NANCY SCHUTT

2

PACK9

a STiTCH iN TiMe

fido™

3

Island Dog Vacations

4

ⅅ = Design Firm ☉ = Client

1A ⅅ Judson Design ☉ Alyssum Klopp 1B ⅅ Extra Point Creative ☉ Kyler Wilson 1C ⅅ Skybend ☉ Web dog
2A ⅅ Sniff Design Studio ☉ Foxy Dog 2B ⅅ Digital Slant ☉ Lead Boy 2C ⅅ View Design Company ☉ Nancy Schutt
3A ⅅ TRUF ☉ pack9 3B ⅅ 13thirtyone Design ☉ A Stitch In Time 3C ⅅ Rome & Gold Creative ☉ Innovasic Semiconductors
4A ⅅ Coleman Creative Design Studio ☉ Island Dog Vacations 4B ⅅ David Barron ☉ Cranston Pet Rehabilitation 4C ⅅ Studio Cue ☉ Yellow Lab, LTD.

A **B** **C**

1

  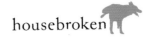

2

3

  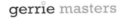 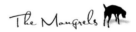

4

Ⓓ = Design Firm Ⓒ = Client

1A Ⓓ co:lab Ⓒ Flagg Road United Church of Christ 1B Ⓓ Funnel Design Group Ⓒ Flip A Do 1C Ⓓ Chris McCampbell Ⓒ House Broken Records
2A Ⓓ ellen bruss design Ⓒ The Lab at Belmar 2B Ⓓ ellen bruss design Ⓒ The Lab at Belmar 2C Ⓓ Lunar Cow Ⓒ Humane Society of Greater Akron
3A Ⓓ Collaboration Reverberation Ⓒ Beckman's Dog Training 3B Ⓓ MacMillan Lynch Ⓒ Gerrie Masters 3C Ⓓ Elevata Ⓒ The Mongrels
4A Ⓓ Blue Clover Ⓒ Huntspace.com 4B Ⓓ Red Clover Studio Ⓒ Airtex Design Group 4C Ⓓ Union Design & Photo Ⓒ In Touch Media Group

A

B

C

1

2

3

4

Ⓓ = Design Firm   Ⓒ = Client

1A Ⓓ Trapdoor Studio Ⓒ The Grand Pet Resort   1B Ⓓ Wonderfuel Ⓒ London Grooming   1C Ⓓ Graphic Moxie, Inc. Ⓒ Three Hounds Gallery
2A Ⓓ dandy idea Ⓒ DogBoy's Dog Ranch   2B Ⓓ Sniff Design Studio Ⓒ Doody Calls   2C Ⓓ WestmorelandFlint Ⓒ Barkhouse Bistro
3A Ⓓ Combustion Ⓒ Verified Person   3B Ⓓ The Netmen Corp Ⓒ Darma Productions   3C Ⓓ Rose/Glenn Group Ⓒ Red Dog
4A Ⓓ Graphic Communication Concepts Ⓒ AIAWA   4B Ⓓ JG Creative Ⓒ JG Creative   4C Ⓓ Toledo Area Metroparks Ⓒ Metroparks of the Toledo Area

A　**B**　**C**

1

2

3

4

D = Design Firm　**C** = Client

1A **D** Off-Leash Studios **C** Off-Leash Studios　1B **D** Red Clover Studio **C** Airtex Design Group　1C **D** Funk/Levis & Associates, Inc.　**C** Dogs at Play

2A **D** Dotzero Design **C** Dotzero　2B **D** TrueBlue, Inc. **C** Cindy Carter　2C **D** mod&co **C** Dog Lovers Night Out

3A **D** Pagliuco Design Company **C** Calypso Systems, Inc.　3B **D** Opolis Design, LLC **C** BuySafe　3C **D** Whaley Design, Ltd **C** Happy Hound Hotel

4A **D** Sniff Design Studio **C** My Dog's Bakery, LLC　4B **D** Thorn Creative **C** Underdog Rescue　4C **D** Guard Dog Brand Development **C** Guard Dog Brand Development

UPTOWN DALLAS DOG PARK

FIVE O`CLOCK
ante meridiem cafe

CASUÉ
WOMAN

1

ACTIVDOG
FOR EVERYDAY ADVENTURES

RUSTY'S
METAL ART

2

SKIPPY DOG
PRODUCTIONS

a. r. f.
ARCHITECTURALLY REFINED FURNITURE

Embark™

3

ZAK & BONES

petswelcome.com

Small Dog
DESIGN
Pty LTD

4

Ⓓ = Design Firm   Ⓒ = Client

1A Ⓓ Squires and Company Ⓒ Uptown Dallas 1B Ⓓ Diagram 1C Ⓓ Simon & Goetz Design Ⓒ HS Fashion
2A Ⓓ Red Clover Studio Ⓒ Airtex Design Group 2B Ⓓ Ryan Graphics Ⓒ Animal Works 2C Ⓓ Dogstar Ⓒ Animal Shelters
3A Ⓓ SwitchStream, LLC Ⓒ Skippy Dog Productions 3B Ⓓ Nanantha Shroff Ⓒ Architecturally Refined Furniture 3C Ⓓ Kurt for Hire Ⓒ Ignite-VP
4A Ⓓ Thinking*Room, Inc. Ⓒ Zak & Bones 4B Ⓓ Zenarts Design Studio Ⓒ Petswelcome.com 4C Ⓓ Small Dog Design Ⓒ Small Dog Design Pty Ltd

A B  C

 1

Yellow Dog Design

 2

 3

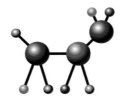

4

D = Design Firm   **C** = Client

1A **D** Stiles Design **C** Fogdog.com   1B **D** Helium Creative, Inc. **C** Island Dogs Bar   1C **D** Yellow Dog Design **C** Yellow Dog Design

2A **D** Entermotion Design Studio **C** Marshmallow Kisses   2B **D** Gee + Chung Design **C** DCM   2C **D** Mike Quon/Designation **C** Designation

3A **D** Univisual **C** Ferplast   3B **D** Beacon Branding, LLC   3C **D** D&i (Design and Image) **C** The Color People

4A **D** Sabingrafik, Inc. **C** K-9 Connection   4B **D** Marc Posch Design, Inc **C** Desiree Snellman   4C **D** The Netmen Corp

A

B

C

1

2

3

4

D = Design Firm   **C** = Client

1A **D** Fine Dog Creative **C** Fur Kids of St. Louis   1B **D** reaves design **C** reaves design   1C **D** UNIT-Y **C** DogBlue
2A **D** Howling Good Designs **C** Mutts and Jeff Dog Training   2B **D** Jane M Illustration **C** Gretchen and Jane Harris
C **D** Howling Good Designs **C** Mutts and Jeff Dog Training   3A **D** 7 Lucky Dogs Creative, LLC **C** Simon and Huey's Doggoned Tasty Treats
3B **D** Chris Rooney Illustration/Design **C** ReputationDefender   3C **D** Joseph Blalock **C** Kong   4A **D** Thorn Creative **C** Well Pet Foods
4B **D** Paragon Design International **C** Buddy Up   4C **D** Shelley Design+Marketing **C** American Cyanamid

A　　　**B**　　　**C**

1

2

3

4

D = Design Firm　　**C** = Client

1A **D** Charles Akins_AkinsTudio **C** That Dirty Dog　1B **D** Dogstar **C** Birmingham Animal Shelter　1C **D** Two Dogs Design **C** Two Dogs Design

2A **D** Green Dog Studio **C** Laundromutt, Inc.　2B **D** Hubbell Design Works **C** Purina Dog Chow　2C **D** Glitschka Studios **C** Color Lab

3A **D** Pix Design, inc. **C** Ellie's K-9 Care　3B **D** Sniff Design Studio **C** House of Hounds　3C **D** Sharisse Steber Design **C** Smooches & Pooches

4A **D** Steve DeCusatis Design　4B **D** Fine Dog Creative **C** Fine Dog Creative　4C **D** Hiebing **C** Dane County Humane Society

A

B

C

PAWS

PAWS

Humane Society
of Greater Akron

COUNCIL
VETERINARY HOSPITAL
HONEST PET CARE

2

Pawsville
when you can't be there yourself

Four Paws
ANIMAL HOSPITAL®

Cesar Millan

3

animal
hotel
MASkargo

4

Ⓓ = Design Firm   Ⓒ = Client

1A Ⓓ Go Media Ⓒ Place a Pet Foundation **1B** Ⓓ Fox Fire Creative Ⓒ Lion Heart **1C** Ⓓ Paragon Marketing Communications Ⓒ PAWS
2A Ⓓ Paragon Marketing Communications Ⓒ PAWS **2B** Ⓓ Lunar Cow Ⓒ Humane Society of Greater Akron **2C** Ⓓ Mohouse Design Co. Ⓒ Council Veterinary Hospital
3A Ⓓ Sabingrafik, Inc. Ⓒ Pawsville **3B** Ⓓ BT Graphics Ⓒ FourPaws Animal Hospital **3C** Ⓓ Copia Creative, Inc. Ⓒ Cesar Millan, Inc.
4A Ⓓ Selikoff+Co Ⓒ West Orange Animal Welfare League **4B** Ⓓ Diana Graham Ⓒ Tierklinik, Diessen, Germany **4C** Ⓓ Arc Worldwide Ⓒ Malaysia Airlines

A   **B**   **C**

1

2

e-dog productions

3

LOST
PUPPY

PRODUCTIONS

B. SPARKS
PHOTOGRAPHER

4

PET ⬦⬦ TOY

D = Design Firm   **C** = Client

1A **D** fuszion **C** Animal Planet   1B **D** Lesniewicz Associates **C** Golden Retriever Rescue of Michigan   1C **D** Steve DeCusatis Design **C** JEG

2A **D** Daniel Sim Design   2B **D** Gardner Design **C** Big Dog Motorcycles   2C **D** R&R Partners **C** Vegas Rock Dog

3A **D** Koodoz Design **C** Lost Puppy Productions   3B **D** RocketDog Communications **C** Bev Sparks Photography   3C **D** switchfoot creative **C** Open Arms Network

4A **D** Joseph Blalock **C** Kong   4B **D** Hubbell Design Works **C** Purina Dog Chow   4C **D** Hubbell Design Works **C** Purina Dog Chow

A

B

C

 1

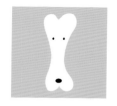

 2

 3

 4

D = Design Firm   **C** = Client

1A **D** Rubber Cheese **C** Big Woolly Dog Productions   **1B** **D** Roskelly, Inc. **C** Charity   **1C** **D** Vestigio—Consultores de Design, Lda. **C** Latido

2A **D** 7981design **C** 7981design   **2B** **D** Cuie&Co **C** Snif Labs   **2C** **D** 903 Creative, LLC **C** Atlantic Animal Hospital

3A **D** The Robin Shepherd Group **C** CatDog Clothing   **3B** **D** Dotzero Design **C** JELD-WEN   **3C** **D** Freshwater Design

4A **D** First Net Impressions, LLC **C** Oakwood Hills Animal Hospital   **4B** **D** Cisneros Design **C** Veterinary Cancer Care   **4C** **D** Calacampania Studios **C** Calagraphic Design

A

B

C

1

Tri-State Animal Emergency Center

fritzy's

2

3

4

D = Design Firm   **C** = Client

1A **D** Beveridge Seay, Inc. **C** Tri-State Animal Emergency Center **1B** **D** bob neace graphic design, inc **C** Kutter Pet Care Center **1C** **D** Fumiko Noon **C** Fritzy's

2A **D** Moss Creative **C** PetsMart **2B** **D** Green Dog Studio **C** Paws & Pose **2C** **D** Heisel Design **C** Wiggles & Giggles

3A **D** Dotzero Design **C** JELD-WEN **3B** **D** Dogstar **C** Animal Shelters **3C** **D** Dogstar **C** Birmingham Animal Shelter

4A **D** Helius Creative Advertising **C** Real Pet Water **4B** **D** Green Dog Studio **C** Fetch it **4C** **D** Boelts Design **C** The Humane Society of Southern Arizona

A

B

C

1

2

3

4

D = Design Firm   **C** = Client

1A **D** Gee Creative **C** Rescue Resource Foundation   1B **D** Felixsockwell.com **C** new york magazine   1C **D** TFI Envision, Inc. **C** Bull's Head Animal Hospital
2A **D** Laurel Black Design, Inc. **C** Best Friend Nutrition   2B **D** Honey Design **C** Two Paws Up   2C **D** This Gunn for Hire **C** Helen Woodward Animal Center
3A **D** The Robin Shepherd Group **C** Rock and Rollover   3B **D** CaliCat Design & Web Consulting **C** Saving Paws Animal Rescue
3C **D** Green Dog Studio **C** The Comfy Critter   4A **D** QueenBee Studio **C** Olde Towne Pet Resort
4B **D** Sussner Design Company **C** animal humane society   4C **D** Evenson Design Group **C** Pet Net

A   **B**   **C**

1       

2       

3    

4       

D = Design Firm   **C = Client**

1A **D** Brandient **C** Domo   1B **D** Sabingrafik, Inc. **C** Dr. Harvey's   1C **D** Diagram **C** Strych z ksiazkami
2A **D** Giorgio Davanzo Design **C** The Dugan Foundation   2B **D** Lynde Design **C** Two Cats Touring   2C **D** moosylvania **C** Purina
3A **D** Gary Sample Design **C** Yesterday's News   3B **D** Extra Point Creative   3C **D** The Drawing Board **C** West Coast Wildcats Baseball
4A **D** Glitschka Studios **C** Robotic Cat Communications   4B **D** Vincent Burkhead Studio **C** Simple Scoop   4C **D** Hip Street

A

B

C

1

2

3

4

D = Design Firm **C** = Client

1A **D** clicketyclick **C** Tabitha London 1B **D** Subcommunication **C** Dj Kobal & Ilya Pauly 1C **D** Westwerk DSGN **C** CatLick Records

2A **D** Westwerk DSGN **C** CatLick Records 2B **D** angryporcupine*design **C** Zombiecat Productions 2C **D** eleven07 **C** SpinSugar Records

3A **D** Jeff Fisher LogoMotives **C** Cat Adoption Team 3B **D** Jerron Ames **C** Arteis 3C **D** Jill Steinfeld : Design Studio **C** Titec USA

4A **D** STUBBORN SIDEBURN **C** Whitworth Elementary School 4B **D** Dotzero Design **C** Sad Sacks and Cats 4C **D** Dirty Design **C** Nouveau Filth

A

B

C

1

bluecat.com

2

PiSHi CLUB

Sharpen your clause.

COPYCAT
WRITING & EDITING

SINGING CAT PRODUCTIONS
Documentary Film & Media

3

HAOS KATT

CAT
Christine Tameena Alix

The Wicked Cafe

4

publicat
GRUPA WYDAWNICZA

SEATTLE CHILDRENS THEATRE

Beekeeper's Cottage
ROMANTIC HOME FURNISHINGS
& ACCESSORIES

D = Design Firm   **C** = Client

1A D Demographic, Inc. **C** Oobiecat Brand **1B D** Patlejch **C** Goran Patlejch **1C D** logobyte **C** BlueCat.com

2A D Sabet Branding **C** Snooki, Inc. **2B D** Riley Designs **C** Copycat Writing and Editing **2C D** Beth Singer Design **C** Singing Cat Productions

3A D orangebird **C** Hauskatt **3B D** baba designs **C** Veritas **3C D** Alana Jelinek Design **C** WICKED CAFE

4A D Diagram **C** Pretext Publishing **4B D** Art Chantry **C** Seattle Childrens Theatre **4C D** yellow dog design **C** Beekeeper's Cottage

A

S E L M A   &   L O U I S

B

FAT CATS

C

TIKEE

1

barncat
PUBLISHING

2

Cat Walk
for the
Cure

GLOW THONG

Simplicity

3

hvsh

CD 101.9

4

Ⓓ = Design Firm   Ⓒ = Client

1A Ⓓ Dreigestalt Ⓒ selma&louis **1B** Ⓓ Boondock Walker Ⓒ Fat Cats Restaurant **1C** Ⓓ Sayles Graphic Design, Inc.

2A Ⓓ Kreatory Studio Ⓒ Kreatory Studio **2B** Ⓓ Special Modern Design Ⓒ Jami Bernard **2C** Ⓓ Entermotion Design Studio Ⓒ Marshmallow Kisses

3A Ⓓ Garza-Allen Designs Ⓒ Ultimate Ventures **3B** Ⓓ BrandExtract Ⓒ Glow Labs **3C** Ⓓ Open Creative Group Ⓒ Simplicity

4A Ⓓ Loop Design Ⓒ Columbia House **4B** Ⓓ Kellum McClain Inc. Ⓒ CD 101.9 **4C** Ⓓ Eagle Imagery Ⓒ Secret Cat Society

A

B

C

1

2

3

4

D = Design Firm   **C** = Client

1A **D** Doink, Inc. **C** Absinthe House Cinemateque   1B **D** meowork intergrated **C** meowork sdn bhd   1C **D** Graphic Communication Concepts **C** AIAWA

2A **D** cypher13 **C** cypher13   2B **D** Richards & Swensen **C** Two Dancing Cats   2C **D** Murillo Design, Inc. **C** Alcatraz

3A **D** tbg design **C** The Owl & The Pussycat   3B **D** Gary Sample Design **C** Sababa Toys   3C **D** Gary Sample Design **C** Sababa Toys

4A **D** Sabingrafik, Inc. **C** Lyon Homes   4B **D** Clockwork Studios **C** Youth Basketball League of Salt Lake City   4C **D** Rickabaugh Graphics **C** Old Dominion University

A

DIORO
MOSAIC

B

C

1

2

MGM
GRAND

RSIIC

ATELIER™

3

SilverDoor

ADVENTURE

4

ⓓ = Design Firm   ⓒ = Client

1A ⓓ Gizwiz Studio ⓒ Dioro Mosaic   1B ⓓ 1310 Studios ⓒ Tomberlin Group   1C ⓓ VanPaul Design ⓒ Allister Cameron

2A ⓓ Sabingrafik, Inc. ⓒ Lincoln Park Zoo   2B ⓓ ONEDRINPEN ⓒ LIONBEAT.COM   2C ⓓ Dotzero Design ⓒ Law Masters

3A ⓓ Canyon Creative ⓒ MGM Grand Hotel and Casino   3B ⓓ Kobalto ⓒ AdStore   3C ⓓ MSI ⓒ Bed, Bath and Beyond

4A ⓓ Gibson ⓒ SilverDoor   4B ⓓ Infiltrate Media ⓒ Gomba Media Solutions   4C ⓓ Mayer Creative ⓒ Tanzania

A   B   C

1

SAVE THE LIONS

JUDAH
C R E A T I V E

DAVIS MONTHAN
Highclass Antitheft Systems

2

BLUE LION
CONSTRUCTION COMPANY

3

LANSOR
deluxe furniture

4

BURLWOOD

Distillerie
FRANCIACORTA
DAL 1901 DISTILLATORI IN FRANCIACORTA

old soul.

D = Design Firm   **C** = Client

1A D Mayer Creative **C** Save the Lions   **1B D** Glitschka Studios **C** Judah Creative   **1C D** RedBrand **C** DavisMonthan

2A D More Branding+Communication **C** PLD Management   **2B D** 314Creative **C** Blue Lion Development Company   **2C D** ezzo Design **C** Feira Internacional de Luanda

3A D Pixélion, LLC **C** Self   **3B D** Pherra **C** Lansor   **3C D** Monster Design Company **C** Sensational Home Staging

4A D CAPSULE **C** Burlwood Financial Group   **4B D** RAINERI DESIGN **C** Distillerie Franciacorta   **4C D** laurendesigns **C** Old Soul Clothing

A **B** **C** **1**

2

3

4

D = Design Firm   **C** = Client

1A **D** Alphabet Arm Design **C** Chris Grosvenor 1B **D** Pavone **C** Epic Technology 1C **D** Endura **C** Kingdom Mission Fund

2A **D** Alphabet Arm Design **C** Jason Young / The Ruse 2B **D** max2o **C** Leeworth Mortgage 2C **D** Rickabaugh Graphics **C** Old Dominion University

3A **D** Pandemonium Creative **C** Pride Performance Group 3B **D** Evenson Design Group **C** MGM 3C **D** Thelogoloft.com **C** Penmark

4A **D** VIVA Creative Group **C** David W. Dick & Associates 4B **D** VanPaul Design **C** Royal Saxon 4C **D** Sabingrafik, Inc.

A **B** **C**

1

2

3

4

D = Design Firm　**C** = Client

1A **D** Burd & Patterson **C** Des Moines Christian School　1B **D** Sabingrafik, Inc. **C** Westmark School　1C **D** Richard Underberg **C** Sigma Alpha Epsilon

2A **D** Matthew Wells Design **C** Kilgore Minerals　2B **D** The Drawing Board **C** WILLIE D.　2C **D** Sabingrafik, Inc. **C** Cranford Group

3A **D** Canyon Creative **C** MGM Grand Hotel and Casino　3B **D** Vivitiv **C** Kindering Center　3C **D** BXC nicelogo.com **C** RastaTaco.com

4A **D** Gardner Design **C** McCoy Realty　4B **D** Grant Currie **C** NZMME　4C **D** RedBrand **C** Ultrasale

A

B

C

BLU LEONE

1

CBCG

**CENTRAL BANK
OF MONTENEGRO**

DONALD ROSS

2

TYÖ- JA ELINKEINOMINISTERIÖ
ARBETS- OCH NÄRINGSMINISTERIET
MINISTRY OF EMPLOYMENT AND THE ECONOMY

J L   M C K I N N E Y
nunquam redondo

3

HARTMAN OIL CO. INC.

Les TiGReS
de LaFaYéTTe

4

Ⓓ = Design Firm   Ⓒ = Client

1A Ⓓ rajasandhu.com Ⓒ Raja Sandhu   1B Ⓓ Sabingrafik, Inc. Ⓒ Wesley School   1C Ⓓ Element Ⓒ Granville Christian Academy
2A Ⓓ Studio GT&P Ⓒ Agraria Ricciolini   2B Ⓓ mIQelangelo Ⓒ Central Bank of Montenegro, contest   2C Ⓓ The Martin Group Ⓒ Donald Ross
3A Ⓓ Porkka & Kuutsa Oy Ⓒ Ministry of Employment and the Economy   3B Ⓓ yarimizoshintaro   3C Ⓓ Federico Rozo Ⓒ Mckinney
4A Ⓓ 360ideas Ⓒ Hartman Oil Co., Inc.   4B Ⓓ MiresBall Ⓒ Deleo Clay Tile Company   4C Ⓓ Prejean Creative Ⓒ Mark Viator

A

B

C

1

2

3

4

D = Design Firm   **C** = Client

1A **D** Insight Design   **C** Cowley College   **1B** **D** Lukatarina   **C** TAE-KWON-DO Klub Tiger   **1C** **D** Lunar Cow   **C** Taming Tigers

2A **D** Bright Strategic Design   **C** Mandalay Pictures   **2B** **D** Studio Simon   **C** Hamilton Tiger-Cats   **2C** **D** Zed+Zed+Eye Creative Communications   **C** Forest High School

3A **D** richard zeid design   **C** Regit, Inc.   **3B** **D** Lisa Wood Design   **C** Roseville, CA   **3C** **D** The Netmen Corp   **C** Snead

4A **D** A3 Design   **C** Tiger Construction   **4B** **D** Harbinger   **C** Tiger Connections   **4C** **D** Studio Simon   **C** Hamilton Tiger-Cats

A

B

C

1

2

3

4

D = Design Firm　**C** = Client

1A **D** DUEL Purpose　**C** Terrel High School　**1B** **D** Fernandez Design　**C** Lincoln Park Zoo　**1C** **D** Epix　**C** Anié Underwear

2A **D** Studio Simon　**C** Hamilton Tiger-Cats　**2B** **D** Trapdoor Studio　**C** Saguaro High School　**2C** **D** MFDI　**C** Tiger Brands, LLC

3A **D** Bounce Design Newcastle Pty Ltd　**C** Transqual　**3B** **D** Glitschka Studios　**C** Brand Navigation, LLC　**3C** **D** Diagram

4A **D** renaud garnier smart rebranding　**C** Ecole Bilingue de Berkeley　**4B** **D** Church Art Works　**C** Judson Middle School　**4C** **D** Thomas Cook Designs　**C** Hair Safari

A

B

C

1

LEOPARD | CO

2

3

4

ⓓ = Design Firm ⓒ = Client

1A ⓓ Born to Design ⓒ Kingsway Christian Church 1B ⓓ DONATELLI+ASSOCIATES ⓒ Lachman Resource Group 1C ⓓ MEGA ⓒ Leopard|co

2A ⓓ 2TREES DESIGN ⓒ Humboldt High School 2B ⓓ 13THFLOOR ⓒ Arctic Cat 2C ⓓ Glitschka Studios ⓒ Creative Company

3A ⓓ Janet Allinger ⓒ Design Animal 3B ⓓ Jason Drumheller ⓒ Frank Family Reunion 3C ⓓ MSI ⓒ Golfsmith

4A ⓓ concussion, llc ⓒ Fort Worth Zoo 4B ⓓ KRE8IVE design ⓒ Saint Ignatius High School 4C ⓓ Rickabaugh Graphics ⓒ New Hampshire Fisher Cats

A	**B**	**C**

   **1**

   **2**

   **3**

   **4**

D = Design Firm   **C** = Client

1A **D** Squires and Company   **C** AeroLynx   1B **D** maximo, inc.   **C** Vehicle Wash Systems   1C **D** Felixsockwell.com   **C** Maplewood High

2A **D** Oluzen   **C** J. Armando Bermudez   2B **D** The Robin Shepherd Group   **C** FunnyFixx.com   2C **D** The Office of Art+Logik   **C** The Wildcat Society

3A **D** Patten ID   **C** Lansing Catholic High School   3B **D** Mike Quon/Designation   **C** Bristol-Myers Squibb   3C **D** MSI   **C** Golfsmith

4A **D** Fernandez Design   **C** Metrowerks   4B **D** maximo, inc.   **C** Vehicle Wash Systems   4C **D** Pennebaker   **C** Presbyterian School

A   **B**   **C**

1

2

3

4

D = Design Firm   **C** = Client

1A **D** Rickabaugh Graphics **C** Cal State, San Marcos   **1B** **D** Jakob Maser Design   **1C** **D** Sabingrafik, Inc. **C** Soil Reliever

2A **D** Robot Creative **C** SecureInfo Corporation   **2B** **D** MSI **C** Golfsmith   **2C** **D** Thinking*Room, Inc. **C** Cork & Screw

3A **D** Glitschka Studios **C** Big Bocca Animation   **3B** **D** Origin Studios **C** Sony Computer Entertainment   **3C** **D** KENNETH DISENO **C** De Remate newspaper

4A **D** Karl Design Vienna **C** Fuchs Books   **4B** **D** DesignWorks Group **C** Greyfox   **4C** **D** Greteman Group

A

B

C

1

2

3

4

D = Design Firm   **C** = Client

1A **D** ANS **C** Zorra Creative   **1B** **D** I Design Creative Group **C** furniturefox.com   **1C** **D** Mitre Agency **C** Sheila Fox

2A **D** Uhlein Design **C** Fox Chase Homeowners Association   **2B** **D** LogoDesignSource.com **C** The Ticket Exchange   **2C** **D** tesser **C** Fox Racing Shox

3A **D** The Netmen Corp **C** Silverfox   **3B** **D** Eagle Imagery **C** TechFox   **3C** **D** TFI Envision, Inc. **C** Ocean Fox Dive Shop

4A **D** Hinge Incorporated **C** The Middleburg Bank   **4B** **D** Trapdoor Studio **C** Rockford Fosgate   **4C** **D** David Clark Design **C** River Spirit Casino

A **B** **C**

1

2

3

4

D = Design Firm **C** = Client

1A D Jason Drumheller **C** Frank Family Reunion **1B D** The Netmen Corp **1C D** Clutch Design **C** Fox Racing, Inc.

2A D mad studios **C** www.badguys.com **2B D** identity studios **2C D** Clockwork Studios **C** Sixman Football Association

3A D Digital Slant **C** Integra Investments **3B D** Matt Whitley **3C D** Zed+Zed+Eye Creative Communications **C** 527th and 1st platoon

4A D Valge Vares **C** Hell Hunt (The Gentle Wolf) **4B D** Paradox Box **C** Ilshat Baiburin **4C D** McGarrah/Jessee **C** Hyatt Regency Lost Pines Resort and Spa

 A

 B

 C

1

J.R.'s TRADING POST

2

PINK COYOTE
clothing

3

COYOTE RIDGE
at Strasburg

Wolf's Pharmacy

4

D = Design Firm   **C** = Client

1A **D** Howling Good Designs **C** Howling Good Designs   1B **D** bartodell.com **C** Ultimate Predator Calls   1C **D** Jones Design **C** J.R.'s Trading Post

2A **D** Digital Slant **C** Blue Coyote Restaurant   2B **D** Digital Slant **C** Blue Coyote Restaurant   2C **D** logobyte **C** Coyote Republic

3A **D** Owen Design **C** Grip Ideas   3B **D** Sabingrafik, Inc. **C** The Buie Family   3C **D** Traction **C** NBA D-League

4A **D** Marketing Art + Science **C** Pauls Homes   4B **D** Peggy Lauritsen Design Group **C** Wolf's Pharmacy   4C **D** Fernandez Design **C** Lincoln Park Zoo

D = Design Firm   **C** = Client

1A **D** Digital Slant   **C** Blue Coyote Restaurant   **1B** **D** Felixsockwell.com   **C** grey dog's coffee   **1C** **D** reaves design   **C** solo Roma

2A **D** Adler & Schmidt Kommunikations-Design   **C** Ziegfeld Marketing Agency   **2B** **D** Dogstar   **C** Billy's Bar and Grill   **2C** **D** faucethead creative   **C** Billy Goat Lawn Service

3A **D** Gardner Design   **C** Hustler   **3B** **D** Gardner Design   **C** Hustler   **3C** **D** Judson Design   **C** Comancherro Wildlife Consultants

4A **D** Mike Quon/Designation   **C** Designation   **4B** **D** Clockwork Studios   **C** Ram Mechanical   **4C** **D** CONCEPTiCONS

1

2

3

4

D = Design Firm   **C** = Client

1A **D** MAIS VEZES / DZIWANI MONTEIRO **C** Impala TI   **1B** **D** Pure Fusion Media **C** Genisys Group   **1C** **D** Tactix Creative
2A **D** GingerBee Creative **C** Montana First Insurance   **2B** **D** Grunt Advertising^Design **C** Grunt Advertising^Design
2C **D** Grunt Advertising^Design **C** Grunt Advertising^Design   **3A** **D** HollanderDesignLab **C** IBEX Integrated   **3B** **D** Sabingrafik, Inc. **C** Cranford Group
3C **D** Sonia Jones Design **C** Nike   **4A** **D** Creative Madhouse **C** Aleutian Eagle Alpacas   **4B** **D** Menikoff Design **C** Drunken Llama   **4C** **D** Zieldesign **C** Jeanne Sharkey

A **B** **C**

1

FALLING CREEK LLAMAS

KIDS LIDS

2

smartwool
REGISTERED TRADEMARK

3

bellwether

SLeep
SANCTUARY

WoolUniforms.com

4

Insomnia
entertainment

FEEDN'
CHLOE

D = Design Firm   **C** = Client

1A **D** Jean Peterson Design **C** Falling Creek Llamas **1B** **D** Church Art Works **C** The Fold Family Ministries **1C** **D** Vanderbyl Design **C** Mountain Lid Woolens

2A **D** Najlon **C** Step Sheep **2B** **D** Dustin Commer **C** INVISTA **2C** **D** Duffy & Partners **C** Smartwool Socks

3A **D** The Netmen Corp **3B** **D** Cisneros Design **C** Sleep Sanctuary **3C** **D** Monkey Paw Studio **C** WoolUniforms.com

4A **D** R&R Partners **C** Insomnia Entertainment **4B** **D** Tomko Design **C** Ditko Design **4C** **D** Dylan Menges **C** BlackSheep Board & Skate

A	B	C	
			**1**
	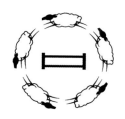		**2**
			**3**
OINK			**4**

ⓓ = Design Firm   ⓒ = Client

1A ⓓ Sternoskop ⓒ Poligraf Publishing **1B** ⓓ reaves design ⓒ reaves design **1C** ⓓ Ross Hogin Design ⓒ Cloud Nine Sheepskin

2A ⓓ Draplin Design Co. ⓒ Gnu Snowboards **2B** ⓓ Morgan/Mohon ⓒ Hiding Place **2C** ⓓ ArtGraphics.ru ⓒ Sherburg

3A ⓓ Sunrise Advertising ⓒ Cincinnati Playhouse in the Park **3B** ⓓ Hubbell Design Works ⓒ Leighton Hubbell **3C** ⓓ Studio3B, Inc. ⓒ Bashert Ministries

4A ⓓ gocreativ ⓒ gocreativ **4B** ⓓ Deep Design ⓒ A Sharper Palate **4C** ⓓ JG Creative ⓒ Salina Art Center Kansas

A　**B**　**C**

1

2

3

4

D = Design Firm　**C** = Client

1A **D** Jill Carson Design **C** Bar and Barbecue　1B **D** PETTUS CREATIVE **C** Dr. Piorkowski　1C **D** Adams & Knight Advertising & Public Relations **C** Art Farm

2A **D** R&R Partners **C** Lopez Industries　2B **D** Panic Creative **C** Secondhand Smokers　2C **D** Sayles Graphic Design, Inc. **C** Iowa State Fair

3A **D** Gary Sample Design　3B **D** Insight Design **C** Carlos O'Kelly's Restaurants　3C **D** 3 Deuces Design, Inc. **C** Phil Duhon

4A **D** D&Dre Creative **C** King Farms　4B **D** Visualink Creative **C** Tennessee BBQ Association　4C **D** The Action Designer **C** Tyslands Kantiner

1

2

3

4

D = Design Firm   **C** = Client

1A **D** Splash:Design **C** The Impeccable Pig Eatery Oinc.   **1B** **D** Amalgamated Studios **C** Caruso Affiliated   **1C** **D** Storm Design, Inc. **C** Mr. Gear Head

2A **D** Mystic Design, Inc. **C** Hoggstyle Productions   **2B** **D** Northfound **C** Pork Barrel BBQ   **2C** **D** Philip J Smith **C** Bowral Brewing Company

3A **D** Muku Studios **C** Flying Pig   **3B** **D** Jeff Fisher LogoMotives **C** Good Pig, Bad Pig   **3C** **D** Range **C** Hogwild Records

4A **D** Karl Design Vienna **C** Pig Bike GmbH   **4B** **D** David Kampa **C** Texas State University Creative Summit   **4C** **D** Gee + Chung Design **C** DCM

 **A**

 **B**

 **C**

1

2

3

4

D = Design Firm **C** = Client

1A **D** Victor Goloubinov **C** First Payment Company **1B** **D** The Netmen Corp **1C** **D** Red Circle **C** Compost-a-mat

2A **D** Mike Quon/Designation **C** Designation **2B** **D** 5 Fifteen Design Group, Inc. **C** Revell Monogram **2C** **D** Rotor Design **C** Kalani Films

3A **D** Steve Cantrell **C** Lance Young, Inc **3B** **D** Redshed Creative Co. **C** Redshed Creative Co. **3C** **D** Q **C** Forsthaus Rheinblick

4A **D** Sauvage Design **C** Antler Developments **4B** **D** Creative NRG **C** Whitetail'R **4C** **D** Simon & Goetz Design **C** adp engineering gmbh/rotwild

A　　　　**B**　　　　**C**

1

2

3

4

D = Design Firm　　**C** = Client

1A **D** Diagram　**1B** **D** Brian Krezel　**C** The Black Heart Project　**1C** **D** Duffy & Partners　**C** The Hockey School

2A **D** julian peck　**2B** **D** Burton (Snowboards) Corp.　**C** Burton Snowboards　**2C** **D** Moss Creative　**C** Houston's Restaurants

3A **D** Diagram　**3B** **D** RIGGS　**C** The Nature Conservancy　**3C** **D** Jennifer Braham Design　**C** Infused Beauty

4A **D** DesignPoint, Inc.　**C** LEMB Co　**4B** **D** Sabingrafik, Inc.　**C** Idyllwilde　**4C** **D** Sabingrafik, Inc.　**C** Marabou

A

B

C

1

2

3

4

ⓓ = Design Firm ⓒ = Client

1A ⓓ Carrihan Creative Group ⓒ Texas Stampede   1B ⓓ Gardner Design ⓒ gardner design   1C ⓓ www.mieland.de

2A ⓓ Zombie Design ⓒ Elk Meadows   2B ⓓ Deep Design ⓒ Macauley Companies   2C ⓓ Miriello Grafico, Inc. ⓒ Harcourt

3A ⓓ Genesis Creative ⓒ Mungo Homes   3B ⓓ adfinity ⓒ DeerCreek Funeral Service   3C ⓓ Randy Mosher Design ⓒ Tom Keith Assoc.

4A ⓓ Church Logo Gallery ⓒ Calvary Church   4B ⓓ TomJon Design Co. ⓒ Piney Holler Hunting Products   4C ⓓ Paper Tower ⓒ Your Future Is Now Ministries

A

B

C

1

2

3

4

D = Design Firm   **C** = Client

1A **D** Christian Rothenhagen **C** deerBLN 1B **D** cc design **C** Kissimmee Billie Swamp Safari 1C **D** Judson Design **C** Hart and Hind Fitness Ranch
2A **D** Frostgiant design firm **C** Fljotsdalsherad 2B **D** Frostgiant design firm **C** Fljotsdalsherad 2C **D** Helius Creative Advertising **C** Kenny Creek Productions
3A **D** Sabingrafik, Inc. **C** Rocky Mountain Elk Foundation 3B **D** 360ideas **C** Elk Ridge 3C **D** Webster Design Associates, Inc. **C** Webster Design
4A **D** DesignPoint, Inc. **C** Adventures West Recreation 4B **D** Digital Slant **C** Moose Mountain Estates 4C **D** Digital Slant **C** Moose Mountain Estates

A

B

C

1

2

3

4

D = Design Firm   **C** = Client

1A **D** Digital Slant **C** Moose Mountain Estates   1B **D** GingerBee Creative   1C **D** Velocity Design Group **C** Expressions

2A **D** Bradshaw Design **C** Moose Winooski's Restaurants   2B **D** Digital Slant **C** Moose Mountain Estates   2C **D** Digital Slant **C** Moose Mountain Estates

3A **D** Rocketman Creative **C** Colts Organization   3B **D** David & Associates **C** Hastings College   3C **D** Razor Creative **C** Mark Crandall

4A **D** Extra Point Creative   4B **D** Clockwork Studios **C** Youth Basketball League of Salt Lake City   4C **D** MFDI **C** Midd-West School District

A **B** **C**

   **1**

   **2**

   **3**

   **4**

D = Design Firm   **C** = Client

1A **D** Pierpoint Design + Branding **C** Douglass Properties   1B **D** Pierpoint Design + Branding **C** Douglass Properties   1C **D** 343 Creative **C** Preferred Equine

2A **D** Richards Brock Miller Mitchell & Associates **C** Magna Entertainment   2B **D** Sabingrafik, Inc. **C** San Dieguito High School

2C **D** Mike Quon/Designation **C** FireCracker Run   3A **D** BadGenius **C** DreamView Stables   3B **D** Glitschka Studios **C** Law Firm

3C **D** Steven O'Connor **C** Law Firm / Cyphon Design   4A **D** Vanderbyl Design   4B **D** Steven O'Connor **C** Open   4C **D** Greteman Group

A   **B**   **C**

1

2

3

4

Eclectia Imports

D = Design Firm   **C** = Client

1A **D** Shelley Design+Marketing **C** The Preakness **1B** **D** Voov Ltd. **C** Aventa Consulting Services
1C **D** Martin Jordan **C** University of Applied Sciences Ostwestfalen-Lippe **2A** **D** Gerard Huerta Design **2B** **D** Sayles Graphic Design, Inc. **C** 3JD **2C** **D** Diagram
3A **D** Rhumb Designs, Inc. **C** Eclectia Imports **3B** **D** switchfoot creative **C** Pacific Performance Horses **3C** **D** Smudge Design Co. **C** The Horse Channel
4A **D** Clover Creative Group, LLC **C** Checkmate Self Defense **4B** **D** mod&co **C** Lucky Seven Horseshoes **4C** **D** Insight Design **C** WorkHorse Recruiting

A **B** **C**

1

2

3

4

D = Design Firm **C** = Client

1A **D** Glitschka Studios **C** Cardwell Creative 1B **D** FIRON **C** Liberty Wind 1C **D** LeBoYe **C** Summarecon Agung, Tbk
2A **D** Fernandez Design **C** Commonwealth of Kentucky 2B **D** LogoDesignSource.com **C** World Barrel Racing Productions
2C **D** GrafiQa Creative Services **C** Fly Creek Friesians 3A **D** Ryder Goodwin **C** Riversong Ranch 3B **D** logobyte 3C **D** Prejean Creative **C** Peninsula Gaming
4A **D** Kreatory Studio **C** Maloo Park 4B **D** Koetter Design **C** Maverick Marketing, LLC 4C **D** Illustra Graphics **C** Mansion Farm

A **B** **C**

1

2

3

4

D = Design Firm **C** = Client

1A **D** Conover **C** Davidson Communities 1B **D** Sabingrafik, Inc. **C** Black Horse Grille 1C **D** TFI Envision, Inc. **C** Sand Castle Farm

2A **D** 5 Fifteen Design Group, Inc. **C** Aquaviva Vineyard and Winery 2B **D** Union Design & Photo **C** Remember this Knight

2C **D** Sparkman + Associates **C** Odyssey International 3A **D** FUEL Creative Group **C** Carmazzi, Inc. 3B **D** VanPaul Design 3C **D** Ulyanov Denis **C** Wit & Wis

4A **D** Elevation Creative Studios **C** Brumfield Hay and Grain 4B **D** Paul Black Design **C** Simon & Schuster 4C **D** Hubbell Design Works **C** Surf & Spa Stables

A

B

C

1

HORUS
CONSULTING

Kristina
Harrison-
Naness

2

3

BLUE MOUNTAIN
RIDING ACADEMY

4

D = Design Firm   **C** = Client

1A **D** Koetter Design **C** Indianapolis Colts   1B **D** Mojo Solo **C** Nuevas Fronteras Spanish Immersion School

1C **D** Pierpoint Design + Branding **C** Douglass Properties   2A **D** Extraverage Productions **C** Horus Consulting   2B **D** Oskoui+Oskoui, Inc. **C** Angele Farms

2C **D** Diana Graham **C** Tierklinik, Diessen, Germany   3A **D** Swanson Russell **C** Purina Mills   3B **D** Richards & Swensen **C** Associate Financial Group

3C **D** creative instinct, inc. **C** Rough Riders   4A **D** Hubbell Design Works **C** Gabel Gawthorpe

4B **D** Tunglid Advertising Agency ehf. **C** Hólar University College   4C **D** The Netmen Corp **C** Blue Mountain

A **B** **C**

1

2

3

4

D = Design Firm   **C** = Client

1A **D** Davidson Branding **C** Victoria Racing Club   **1B** **D** Stiles Design **C** Half Moon Farm   **1C** **D** Bonilla Design **C** Arlington Park Racecourse

2A **D** Page Design **C** Capitol Harness Racing at Cal Expo   **2B** **D** SK+G Advertising **C** Borgata, AC   **2C** **D** Double Brand **C** Poznan International Fair

3A **D** DesignLingo **C** Jockey Management Group   **3B** **D** Richards Brock Miller Mitchell & Associates **C** Lone Star Park   **3C** **D** Prejean Creative **C** Peninsula Gaming

4A **D** Boelts Design **C** Polo Event   **4B** **D** Letterhead Design Studio **C** RDN Real Estate   **4C** **D** Braue: Brand Design Experts **C** La Stalla Ristorante

A

B

C

1

2

3

4

D = Design Firm   **C** = Client

1A **D** Grunt Advertising^Design **C** Grunt Advertising^Design   **1B** **D** Switch Branding & Design **C** The Gauteng Horse Society   **1C** **D** Glitschka Studios **C** Cardwell Creative

2A **D** Green Ink Studio **C** Cavalry Insurance Services   **2B** **D** Sayles Graphic Design, Inc. **C** Berrington Marble   **2C** **D** Crain Associates **C** Laurence Merritt

3A **D** mugur mihai **C** Blum & Silver   **3B** **D** Meir Billet Ltd. **C** Defensive Shield   **3C** **D** Monigle Associates, Inc. **C** WilTel Communiations Systems, Inc.

4A **D** Extra Point Creative **C** University of Central Florida   **4B** **D** Delikatessen **C** Brau und Brunnen

4C **D** Visual Coolness **C** Ruiz Engineering/Las Villas de Kino Apartment Homes

A **B** **C**

1

2

3

4

D = Design Firm   **C** = Client

1A **D** Clockwork Studios   **C** KLRN public television   1B **D** Pinnacle Design Center   **C** Peter & John Radio Fellowship   1C **D** Hill Design Studios   **C** Hill Design Studios

2A **D** Arsenal Design, Inc.   **C** Wild West Ice Cream Company   2B **D** RJ Thompson   **C** Hillview Tavern   2C **D** Sabingrafik, Inc.   **C** McMillin Homes

3A **D** Ground Zero Communications   **C** Kicking Horse Lodges   3B **D** Page Design   **C** Jackknife Creek Ranch   3C **D** Union Design & Photo   **C** Equipment Corral

4A **D** Schuster Design Group   **C** Blockbuster   4B **D** Sabingrafik, Inc.   **C** The Buie Family   4C **D** S Design, Inc.   **C** Looper Brand

1

2

3

4

D = Design Firm   **C** = Client

1A D WestmorelandFlint **C** Bobcat **1B D** Jon Flaming Design **C** Cattle Baron's **1C D** Insight Design **C** Aussie Beef

2A D Chimera Design **C** Falls Creek Board of Management **2B D** Jacq Design, LLC **C** Flying Horse Farms **2C D** Torch Creative **C** Collegiate Licensing Company

3A D 7981design **C** 7981design **3B D** Sabingrafik, Inc. **C** Seaport Village **3C D** Sabingrafik, Inc. **C** Seaport Village

4A D Alien Identity **C** Rocking J&R Ranch **4B D** R&R Partners **C** Patty Zimmer **4C D** Airtype Studio **C** Buckybay

A   **B**   **C**

 1

 2

3

 4

D = Design Firm   **C** = Client

1A **D** Carmi e Ubertis Milano Srl **C** Gilberti Giocattoli   **1B** **D** fuszion **C** Madison Hotels   **1C** **D** 1 Trick Pony **C** 1 Trick Pony

2A **D** Hinge **C** Loudoun County Chamber of Commerce   **2B** **D** Hubbell Design Works **C** Sundance Farms   **2C** **D** Grunt Advertising^Design **C** Grunt Advertising^Design

3A **D** GodwinGroup **C** KLLM Transport   **3B** **D** Hot Dog Design **C** Dundalk 5   **3C** **D** Digital Slant **C** Shundahai

4A **D** Bystrom Design **C** Toscana Builders   **4B** **D** Marketing Art + Science **C** Norstar Residential   **4C** **D** 1310 Studios **C** Stone Horse Imports

1

2

3

4

D = Design Firm **C** = Client

1A D Purple Zante, Inc.   **1B D** Phixative **C** DragonHorse International   **1C D** A3 Design **C** mattamy homes   **2A D** Fuzzy Duck Design **C** Canterbury Storage
2B D Sabingrafik, Inc. **C** McMillin Homes   **2C D** Metropolis Advertising **C** Marriott   **3A D** Sabingrafik, Inc. **C** Weathervanes Unlimited
3B D Dennard, Lacey & Associates **C** Light Farms   **3C D** E. Tage Larsen Design **C** Sixteen Three   **4A D** Communication Arts **C** Magna Entertainment Corporation
4B D Macnab Design **C** Maddoux Arabian Horse Farm   **4C D** Tunglid Advertising Agency ehf. **C** Skálakot

1

A

B

C

2

EVERGREEN
equine veterinary practice

AIDA JOHANNES
DRESSAGE

3

4

D = Design Firm **C** = Client

1A **D** MINE(tm) **C** Jim Mitchell 1B **D** Hubbell Design Works **C** In the Hunt Farm 1C **D** Digital Flannel **C** Okemo

2A **D** Nynas **C** Running Aces 2B **D** Paul Svancara **C** Evergreen Equine Veterinary Practice 2C **D** Woodend, Nessel & Friends **C** Aida Johannes

3A **D** Graves Fowler Creative **C** National Apartment Association 3B **D** Hornall Anderson **C** Twelve Horses 3C **D** 343 Creative **C** 3 Boros Communications

4A **D** Studio Simon **C** East Texas Pump Jacks 4B **D** Hula+Hula **C** Mula 4C **D** Brian Krezel **C** Kicking Mule Workshop

A

B

C

1

2

3

4

D = Design Firm   **C** = Client

1A **D** Glitschka Studios   **C** Templin Brink Design   **1B** **D** Grapefruit   **C** Softouch   **1C** **D** Felixsockwell.com   **C** New York Times

2A **D** Charles Design   **C** White Buffalo Entertainment   **2B** **D** McQuillen Creative Group   **C** Dakota Scrubbers   **2C** **D** bob neace graphic design, inc   **C** KGA

3A **D** Greteman Group   **3B** **D** Oxide Design Co.   **C** Nebraska AIDS Project   **3C** **D** David Clark Design   **C** River Spirit Casino

4A **D** The Joe Bosack Graphic Design Co.   **C** Bucknell University   **4B** **D** Blue Clover   **C** City of Cibolo   **4C** **D** bob neace graphic design, inc   **C** Mid American Credit Union

A **B** **C**

1

2

3

4

D = Design Firm   **C** = Client

1A **D** Barnstorm Creative Group, Inc **C** Canadian Football League   1B **D** David Meyer Studio **C** Buffalo River Films   1C **D** 13THFLOOR **C** Pro-Tec / Mosa

2A **D** MSI **C** Products Direct   2B **D** R&R Partners **C** Luxor Las Vegas   2C **D** R&R Partners **C** Southern Nevada Water Authority

3A **D** MSI **C** Products Direct   3B **D** MSI **C** Products Direct   3C **D** Brickhouse Creative

4A **D** GCG **C** Fort Worth Opera   4B **D** Judson Design **C** Yellow Bike Project   4C **D** RADAR Agency **C** Texas Department of Agriculture

A

B

C

1

2

3

4

D = Design Firm   **C** = Client

1A **D** Turnstyle   **C** Matador   **1B** **D** The Logo Factory, Inc.   **C** Dirty West Entertainment   **1C** **D** Visible Ink Design   **C** Outback Traders Australia

2A **D** Friends University   **C** Country Stampede   **2B** **D** HMK Archive   **C** Mission Road Development Center   **2C** **D** Felixsockwell.com   **C** los angeles magazine

3A **D** Dotzero Design   **C** Boise Paper   **3B** **D** The Netmen Corp   **3C** **D** VanPaul Design   **C** The University of Texas

4A **D** Bluespace Creative(r), Inc.   **C** The Bull, inc.   **4B** **D** Doink, Inc.   **C** Burger King   **4C** **D** Sabingrafik, Inc.   **C** Maddox Design

A **B** **C**

1

2

3

4

D = Design Firm **C** = Client

1A D Tactix Creative **C** Splendid Seed **1B D** Jeff Kern Design **1C D** Mike Quon/Designation **C** Designation

2A D thackway+mccord **C** Rio Restaurant **2B D** Haller Design **2C D** El Paso, Galeria de Comunicacion **C** Taurobulia

3A D Sussner Design Company **C** Cafe Europa **3B D** dache **C** Brokers **3C D** The Netmen Corp

4A D Zeiber Design **C** BlueBrahma.com **4B D** PUSH Branding and Design **C** Blue Ribbon Prime Steakhouse **4C D** Sabingrafik, Inc. **C** Cranford Group

A	B	C

1

2

3

4

ⅅ = Design Firm Ⅽ = Client

1A ⅅ Digital Flannel Ⅽ Okemo 1B ⅅ Digital Flannel Ⅽ Okemo 1C ⅅ Sabingrafik, Inc. Ⅽ Farmlinks, LLC

2A ⅅ Gyula Nemeth Ⅽ Everlast 2B ⅅ Rickabaugh Graphics Ⅽ Texas Longhorns 2C ⅅ Rickabaugh Graphics Ⅽ Texas Longhorns

3A ⅅ Gyula Nemeth Ⅽ Axel-Springer 3B ⅅ Gary Sample Design 3C ⅅ max2o Ⅽ American Cancer Society

4A ⅅ Rickabaugh Graphics Ⅽ Oklahoma State University 4B ⅅ dandy idea Ⅽ The Retreat at CandleLight Ranch 4C ⅅ David Kampa Ⅽ ProTrader

A **B** **C**

1

2

3

4

Ⓓ = Design Firm   Ⓒ = Client

1A Ⓓ alloy studio Ⓒ Pearce Brothers Meats   **1B** Ⓓ Thomas Cook Designs Ⓒ Medium Rare Software   **1C** Ⓓ DUSTIN PARKER ARTS Ⓒ EL DIGERATI

2A Ⓓ WhiteRhino Creative PL Ⓒ TiedUp   **2B** Ⓓ Entropy Brands Ⓒ Montana Beef & Game Company   **2C** Ⓓ S&N Design Ⓒ So Long Saloon

3A Ⓓ Sabingrafik, Inc. Ⓒ Farmlinks, LLC   **3B** Ⓓ paralleldesigned Ⓒ Cornerstone Management Group   **3C** Ⓓ Kym Abrams Design Ⓒ IDA Advisors

4A Ⓓ Archrival Ⓒ Kicking Cow   **4B** Ⓓ Hirschmann Design Ⓒ Hidden Rock Ranch   **4C** Ⓓ Strange Ideas

1

2

3

4

D = Design Firm   **C** = Client

1A **D** Mohouse Design Co. **C** M & O Cattle Co. **1B** **D** David Kampa **C** Beef & Pie Productions **1C** **D** Entermotion Design Studio **C** Palomino Foods

2A **D** ADC Global Creativity **C** Ganaderos Productores de Leche Pura S.A. de C.U. **2B** **D** Kat & Mouse Graphic Design **C** Madcow

2C **D** Willoughby Design Group **C** Sheridan's Lattés and Frozen Custard

3A **D** Studio IX OPUS ADA **C** kultivator **3B** **D** Boondock Walker **3C** **D** Banowetz + Company, Inc. **C** Moo Cheeses, L.P.

4A **D** David Gramblin **C** MUE **4B** **D** Glitschka Studios **C** ReThink Communications **4C** **D** Saturn Flyer **C** Saturn Flyer

1

A

B

C

2

3

4

D = Design Firm   **C** = Client

1A **D** Glitschka Studios **C** ReThink Communications   **1B** **D** David Maloney **C** David Maloney   **1C** **D** Insight Design **C** Swan Brothers Dairy, Inc.

2A **D** Mark Oliver, Inc. **C** Bellwether Farm   **2B** **D** sarah watson design **C** Muzzall Farms   **2C** **D** Miriello Grafico, Inc. **C** Mootown Creamery

3A **D** Hubbell Design Works **C** Lyon Homes   **3B** **D** The Netmen Corp **C** My Local Cause   **3C** **D** Ivey McCoig Creative Partners **C** Good Stuff Eatery

4A **D** Westwerk DSGN **C** Bite, Ltd   **4B** **D** Stacy Bormett Design, LLC **C** Ideation Factory   **4C** **D** Lindedesign **C** Milk My Music

1

2

3

4

ⅅ = Design Firm ⅭＣ = Client

1A ⅅ Brook Group, LTD Ⅽ Rob Krupicka   1B ⅅ Graphic D-Signs, Inc. Ⅽ ChocolateMarketplace.com   1C ⅅ Lunar Cow Ⅽ Lunar Cow

2A ⅅ Nubson Design Ⅽ Over the Moon Books   2B ⅅ Torch Creative Ⅽ Javalato   2C ⅅ CAPSULE Ⅽ Schroeder Milk

3A ⅅ Barnstorm Creative Group, Inc Ⅽ Coast Mountain Sports   3B ⅅ Tactix Creative Ⅽ 3inaBox.com   3C ⅅ ellen bruss design Ⅽ Marczyk Fine Foods

4A ⅅ brandStrata Ⅽ Stuart Anderson's   4B ⅅ Exhibit A: Design Group Ⅽ Two Rivers Specialty Meats   4C ⅅ Diagram Ⅽ Sano

A **B** **C**

1

2

3

4

D = Design Firm   **C** = Client

1A **D** Extra Point Creative   1B **D** R&R Partners   **C** MGM   1C **D** Extra Point Creative

2A **D** The Joe Bosack Graphic Design Co.   **C** Drew University   2B **D** RARE Design   **C** NBA   2C **D** RARE Design   **C** NBA

3A **D** Draplin Design Co.   **C** Minneapolis College of Art + Design   3B **D** GrafiQa Creative Services   3C **D** Kiku Obata & Company   **C** Boca Bear Foods

4A **D** Thirtythr33   4B **D** helium.design   **C** Arndt Kresse   4C **D** Strange Ideas

1

2

3

4

ⅅ = Design Firm   ⅭⓁ = Client

1A ⅅ Sebastiany Branding & Design Ⓒ Panda Stock 1B ⅅ Paradox Box Ⓒ City administration 1C ⅅ Carrihan Creative Group Ⓒ BearNotes

2A ⅅ KW43 BRANDDESIGN Ⓒ Ritzenhoff AG 2B ⅅ Mitre Agency Ⓒ Mental Health Association 2C ⅅ Lienhart Design Ⓒ Chicago 27 Designers

3A ⅅ SUPERRED Ⓒ Plush beauty salon 3B ⅅ RK Design Ⓒ Zendy 3C ⅅ volatile-graphics

4A ⅅ Whaley Design, Ltd Ⓒ Business Incentives, Inc. 4B ⅅ Tactix Creative Ⓒ Burly Bear TV 4C ⅅ Gardner Design Ⓒ Kroger

A B C

 1

 2

3

 4

D = Design Firm   C = Client

1A D Kinesis, Inc. C Providence Medford Medical Center   **1B** D ADC Global Creativity C Bimbo Bakeries   **1C** D Device

2A D Entropy Brands C Little Angel Nursery   **2B** D Straka-Design C Kinderkram (Second Hand Toys)   **2C** D Spela Draslar C Ardis, d.o.o.

3A D c3 C Corporate Id   **3B** D Webster Design Associates, Inc. C Ted E. Bear Hollow   **3C** D Chris Rooney Illustration/Design C Shea Homes

4A D 2B Design C Beardsley Zoo   **4B** D Sabingrafik, Inc. C Sabingrafik, Inc.   **4C** D Hill Aevium C Town of Vail

A **B** **C**

1

2

3

4

D = Design Firm   **C** = Client

1A **D** Glitschka Studios **C** Advanced Refrigeration & Air   1B **D** Blattner Brunner **C** Pittsburgh Zoo & PPG Aquarium   1C **D** Nynas **C** Polarity Club
2A **D** Glitschka Studios **C** Advanced Refrigeration & Air   2B **D** Rusty George Creative **C** Point Defiance Zoo & Aquarium
2C **D** Fandam Studio **C** Black Bear Resources, Ltd.   3A **D** Thomas Cook Designs **C** Klondike Cafe   3B **D** Strange Ideas   3C **D** Smith Design **C** Unilever
4A **D** The Joe Bosack Graphic Design Co. **C** Alaska Aces   4B **D** Chris Rooney Illustration/Design **C** Shea Homes   4C **D** William Herod Design **C** BearzeeZ

A　　　**B**　　　**C**

 1

 2

3

 4

D = Design Firm　**C** = Client

1A **D** Idea Girl Design **C** Let's take five　1B **D** M3 Advertising Design **C** PSI Seminars—Las Vegas　1C **D** Bulldog & Braun

2A **D** Greteman Group　2B **D** Diagram **C** BSR　2C **D** Squires and Company **C** Bear Dance Spas

3A **D** Rick Carlson Design & Illustration **C** Rick Carlson　3B **D** Studio grafickih ideja **C** Croatian Ski Association　3C **D** STUBBORN SIDEBURN **C** Furry Pocket Factory

4A **D** Sabingrafik, Inc. **C** Treasure State Bank　4B **D** Vanderbyl Design **C** Bedford Art Publishing　4C **D** AKOFA Creative **C** Self-Promotional

Durflinger Homes

Red Bear Café

1

CIVIL JUSTICE ASSOCIATION
OF
CALIFORNIA

2

Kelowna
Museums

3

4

D = Design Firm **C** = Client

1A **D** BLAM, Inc. **C** Durflinger Homes **1B** **D** Peterson & Company **C** George Fox University **1C** **D** GrafiQa Creative Services

2A **D** Archrival **C** Civil Justice Association of California **2B** **D** Rickabaugh Graphics **C** Baylor University **2C** **D** Rickabaugh Graphics **C** Morgan State University

3A **D** Object 9 **C** Baton Rouge Community College **3B** **D** Studio Simon **C** New Britain Rock Cats **3C** **D** Splash:Design **C** Kelowna Museums

4A **D** The Logo Factory, Inc. **C** Buena Vista University **4B** **D** Sayles Graphic Design, Inc. **C** Buena Vista University **4C** **D** Sayles Graphic Design, Inc. **C** Beaver Mower

1

HALF BADGER
R E C O R D S

2

moneta
porcupine
EST. 1910

3

4

D = Design Firm   **C** = Client

1A **D** Studiofluid **C** Half Badger Records 1B **D** Rickabaugh Graphics **C** University of Wisconsin 1C **D** Gridwerk **C** Union League Philadelphia
2A **D** Rackel Creative **C** Moneta Porcupine Mines 2B **D** WhiteRhino Creative PL **C** Vital Software 2C **D** Glitschka Studios **C** Bartow County Georgia
3A **D** Via Grafik **C** bstrkt industries 3B **D** About350, Inc. **C** Save Our Skunks 3C **D** XY ARTS
4A **D** Simple Creative Design **C** Clever Mink's 4B **D** Design Outpost **C** batcave.net 4C **D** 360ideas

A **B** **C**

1

2

3

4

D = Design Firm   **C** = Client

1A **D** lis design **C** Aardvark Pet Sitting   **1B** **D** artbox studios **C** Arts Conservatory of Central Pennsylvania   **1C** **D** Pixel Boy Studio **C** Stand Alone, Inc.

2A **D** Saltree Pty Ltd **C** Harding Estate   **2B** **D** United States of the Art **C** Carlo Krüger   **2C** **D** eggnerd **C** Team Roadkill

3A **D** eggnerd **C** Team Roadkill   **3B** **D** Platform Creative Group **C** Armadillo   **3C** **D** Alphabet Arm Design **C** Alphabet Arm

4A **D** Mike Quon/Designation **C** Clairol   **4B** **D** Michael Patrick Partners **C** The Otter Run   **4C** **D** Sabingrafik, Inc. **C** Sabingrafik, Inc.

A B C

D = Design Firm   **C** = Client

1A **D** Nissen Design   **C** Tom Festival   **1B** **D** Extra Point Creative   **C** Jason Milke   **1C** **D** McArtor Design   **C** Community Savings Bank

2A **D** Gary Sample Design   **C** In Abundance   **2B** **D** LeBoYe   **C** Puri Tupai   **2C** **D** The Logo Factory, Inc.   **C** Dygo Search

3A **D** Device   **3B** **D** Eskil Ohlsson Assoc. Inc.   **C** Kelling Nut Co.   **3C** **D** Greteman Group   **C** Greteman Group Client Gift

4A **D** Fons Schiedon   **C** Submarinechannel.com   **4B** **D** Creative Beard   **C** Culture Pop Clothing   **4C** **D** Mike Quon/Designation   **C** Designation

A

B

C

1

2

3

4

D = Design Firm   C = Client

1A **D** Simon & Goetz Design **C** sieger design/ritzenhoff   1B **D** LSD **C** un mundo feliz / a happy world production   1C **D** Strategy Studio **C** Strategy Studio

2A **D** Fuze **C** Bobo's   2B **D** Jeff Kern Design **C** Apple Pie Entertainment—Robison Creative Studios   2C **D** Artnak **C** Slon in Sadez

3A **D** Chip Sheean **C** Walt Disney Records   3B **D** Jason Kochis **C** Meeshko Toys   3C **D** Stiles Design **C** MouseCloud

4A **D** Fuze **C** Bobo's   4B **D** Sabingrafik, Inc. **C** University of California, San Diego   4C **D** Jeff Kern Design **C** XMice—3 Floors

A **B** **C**

1

2

3

4   Hugh Heiner
SKY VILLA

D = Design Firm **C** = Client

1A **D** Glitschka Studios **C** Thug Bunny **1B** **D** United States of the Art **C** Carsten Raffel **1C** **D** Skybend **C** Happy Rabbit

2A **D** United States of the Art **C** Carsten Raffel **2B** **D** United States of the Art **C** Carsten Raffel **2C** **D** Cabbage Design Company **C** Anjel Van Slyke

3A **D** helium.design **C** helium.design **3B** **D** Shawn Huff **C** Dustin Huff **3C** **D** Carrihan Creative Group **C** Arcane Tees

4A **D** Mike Quon/Designation **C** Designation **4B** **D** Jerron Ames **C** Arteis **4C** **D** Kurt Snider Design **C** Palms Resort Casino

A

B

C

1

2

Bunnyfly

3

4

ⓓ = Design Firm   ⓒ = Client

1A ⓓ Jackrabbit Design ⓒ Jackrabbit Design   1B ⓓ Richards Brock Miller Mitchell & Associates ⓒ Williamson Printing Company
1C ⓓ BDG STUDIO RONIN ⓒ Utopia for Greater Baltimore Technology Council
2A ⓓ The Netmen Corp ⓒ Tainted   2B ⓓ United States of the Art ⓒ Carsten Raffel   2C ⓓ dk design ⓒ Six Flags over Texas
3A ⓓ Digital Flannel ⓒ VT Ski Museum   3B ⓓ McGarrah/Jessee ⓒ Hyatt Regency Lost Pines Resort and Spa   3C ⓓ Diagram
4A ⓓ Moosylvania ⓒ Moosylvania   4B ⓓ Effective Media Solutions   4C ⓓ Shawn Huff ⓒ Mildred Clement

1

2

3

4

Ⓓ = Design Firm Ⓒ = Client

1A Ⓓ Welcome Moxie Ⓒ Bunny **1B** Ⓓ TFI Envision, Inc. Ⓒ Hilltop **1C** Ⓓ Hubbell Design Works Ⓒ Will Hare Photography

2A Ⓓ Gardner Design Ⓒ Hustler **2B** Ⓓ Gardner Design Ⓒ Hustler **2C** Ⓓ Dogstar Ⓒ Hare Advertising

3A Ⓓ Emerge Design Group Ⓒ Self Promo **3B** Ⓓ ginger griffin marketing and design Ⓒ Custom Creation Embroidery **3C** Ⓓ Karl Design Vienna Ⓒ Hasler AG (proposal)

4A Ⓓ Gardner Design Ⓒ Hustler **4B** Ⓓ Entermotion Design Studio Ⓒ MoJack **4C** Ⓓ Janet Allinger Ⓒ Laurie Proscia, Therapist

A	B	C

1

2

3

4

D = Design Firm **C** = Client

1A **D** Ines Shih 1B **D** Walsh Branding **C** Dovetail Rabbit 1C **D** Dotzero Design **C** Queen of Sheba

2A **D** McDougall & Duval Advertising **C** Anna Jaques Hospital 2B **D** RADAR Agency **C** Ag Commissioner Todd Staples 2C **D** Silver Creative Group **C** the Kingsley Giraffe

3A **D** Giraffe, Inc. **C** Giraffe, Inc. 3B **D** Red Dog Design Consultants **C** Giraffe Childcare 3C **D** Small Dog Design **C** UFS Dispensaries

4A **D** Fernandez Design **C** Lincoln Park Zoo 4B **D** BrandLogic **C** BrandLogic 4C **D** WONGDOODY **C** Woodland Park Zoo

D = Design Firm   **C** = Client

1A D Studio grafickih ideja **C** 0800Dostava   **1B D** Design Hovie Studios, Inc. **C** Zebra Hill Marketing   **1C D** M3 Advertising Design **C** Ameristar Casinos

2A D Studio Simon **C** SUNY Canton   **2B D** reaves design **C** yellow tail   **2C D** Jonathan Rice & Company **C** Capital One

3A D The Joe Bosack Graphic Design Co. **C** University of Akron   **3B D** Brown Ink Design **C** Austral Bricks   **3C D** Daniel Sim Design

4A D The Netmen Corp   **4B D** The Logo Factory, Inc.   **4C D** Brandient **C** Metropotam

A · B · C

1

2

3

4

Ⓓ = Design Firm   Ⓒ = Client

1A Ⓓ BXC nicelogo.com Ⓒ William Scott Brewing Co.   **1B** Ⓓ Clockwork Studios Ⓒ Sixman Football Association   **1C** Ⓓ Mindgruve Ⓒ Rhino Linings
2A Ⓓ Hubbell Design Works Ⓒ Amcoat Technologies   **2B** Ⓓ Sabingrafik, Inc. Ⓒ Tamansari Beverage   **2C** Ⓓ Built Creative Ⓒ K&G Builders
3A Ⓓ Storm Design, Inc. Ⓒ Rhino Waste Management   **3B** Ⓓ concussion, llc Ⓒ Fort Worth Zoo   **3C** Ⓓ BrainBox Studio Ⓒ Boepens Biltong S.A.
4A Ⓓ Sabingrafik, Inc. Ⓒ Beithan Hessler Corporate Communications   **4B** Ⓓ www.mieland.de Ⓒ PYADES Technologies   **4C** Ⓓ Moss Creative Ⓒ Houston's Restaurants

	A	B	C

1

2

3

4

Ⓓ = Design Firm   Ⓒ = Client

1A Ⓓ Sayles Graphic Design, Inc. Ⓒ Rhino Materials   1B Ⓓ Glitschka Studios Ⓒ White Rhino Productions   1C Ⓓ Ground Zero Communications Ⓒ Excallibur Pallets

2A Ⓓ M3 Advertising Design Ⓒ Frank Mistretta   2B Ⓓ orton design Ⓒ blake mcwillis   2C Ⓓ Studio Simon Ⓒ Modesto A's

3A Ⓓ Gardner Design Ⓒ Allied Crane   3B Ⓓ plus1 Ⓒ Elephant Motorsports   3C Ⓓ 343 Creative Ⓒ HSBC Private Bank

4A Ⓓ Maycreate Ⓒ Mammoth Data   4B Ⓓ Sternoskop Ⓒ Poligraf Publishing   4C Ⓓ Gardner Design Ⓒ MegaFab Corporation

1

2

ISTOČNA ČUDA

3

al2r ego

4

ⅅ = Design Firm   ⅭⅭ = Client

1A ⅅ Tom Martin Design Ⅽ XL Media   1B ⅅ www.dannygiang.com Ⅽ 01d Ⅽ Moscow Business School
2A ⅅ RADAR Agency Ⅽ Fort Worth Republican Women   2B ⅅ Felixsockwell.com Ⅽ gop100   2C ⅅ die Transformer Ⅽ Maximilian Park
3A ⅅ VanPaul Design Ⅽ Getamover.com   3B ⅅ Delikatessen Ⅽ Baby Elephant   3C ⅅ vladimir sijerkovic Ⅽ Istocna Cuda—Eastern Miracles
4A ⅅ Lightship Visual Ⅽ Hidden Shoal Recordings   4B ⅅ Webster Design Associates, Inc. Ⅽ Webster Design   4C ⅅ Daniel Sim Design Ⅽ Safari Tan

A   **B**   **C**

1

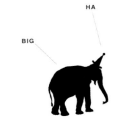

2

3

4

D = Design Firm   **C** = Client

1A **D** Sandstrom Partners **C** Bigha   1B **D** yarimizoshintaro   1C **D** Ross Hogin Design **C** Big Picture Creative

2A **D** Carol Gravelle Graphic Design **C** Wildlife Friendly Enterprise Network   2B **D** TFI Envision, Inc. **C** Living with Elephants Foundation

2C **D** Carrihan Creative Group **C** Carrihan Creative Group   3A **D** monkeebox, inc. **C** monkeebox, inc   3B **D** Glitschka Studios **C** Ascending Technologies

3C **D** reaves design **C** monkeyonacupcake.com   4A **D** Rule29 **C** Rule29   4B **D** dache **C** hired monkey   4C **D** Miaso Design **C** Monkey Media

A　　　　B　　　　C

1

2

3

4

D = Design Firm　　**C** = Client

1A **D** Lindedesign **C** Alive　**1B** **D** Patten ID **C** Monkeywise Marketing　**1C** **D** Patten ID **C** JUJU Jewelry

2A **D** Boelts Design **C** Nimbus Brewery　**2B** **D** Trapdoor Studio **C** Monkey Depot　**2C** **D** DTM_INC **C** Blue Monkeys

3A **D** Extra Point Creative **C** Whiskey Chimp Apparel Co.　**3B** **D** Extra Point Creative **C** Whiskey Chimp band　**3C** **D** Extra Point Creative **C** Whiskey Chimp band

4A **D** Access Media Lab **C** Access Media Lab　**4B** **D** DONATELLI+ASSOCIATES **C** Blue Monkey Theater Co.

4C **D** tomvasquez.com **C** The Black Eyed Peas/ A&M Records

A **B** **C**

1

2

3

4

D = Design Firm **C** = Client

1A **D** BrandExtract **C** Stripes Convenience Stores **1B** **D** MiresBall **C** QUALCOMM **1C** **D** Sayles Graphic Design, Inc. **C** Sayles Graphic Design
2A **D** Simon & Goetz Design **C** factor product **2B** **D** Madden **C** Sweat Monkey **2C** **D** NOMADESIGN, Inc. **C** The Monkey Tavern
3A **D** Popgun **C** Bonny Doon **3B** **D** Same Key Design **C** Chimpanzee Collaboratory **3C** **D** oakley design studios **C** red monkey ads & ideas
4A **D** Sussner Design Company **C** Joe Schaak **4B** **D** Thielen Designs **C** Manic Monkee Management **4C** **D** The Netmen Corp

A

B

C

1

2

3

4

Ⓓ = Design Firm Ⓒ = Client

1A Ⓓ Jeremy Stott Ⓒ Arteis 1B Ⓓ Lindedesign 1C Ⓓ Lukatarina Ⓒ Katarina Mrvar

2A Ⓓ Jeremy Stott Ⓒ Arteis 2B Ⓓ Dennard, Lacey & Associates Ⓒ Samango Software, LLC 2C Ⓓ Zachary Bruno Baltimore Creative Ⓒ Cheeky Monkey Copy

3A Ⓓ Tomko Design Ⓒ Ditko Design 3B Ⓓ Sabingrafik, Inc. Ⓒ Tamarindo Diria 3C Ⓓ Douglas Beatty Ⓒ Bad Monkey Bead Company

4A Ⓓ Fire Monkey Design Studio Ⓒ Fire Monkey Design Studio 4B Ⓓ Flying Chicken Studios Ⓒ Moving Adventures 4C Ⓓ reaves design Ⓒ Will Eikleberry Guitars

A **B** **C**

1

2

3

4

D = Design Firm   **C** = Client

1A **D** DUSTIN PARKER ARTS **C** The Dark Scientists **1B** **D** Estudio Ray **C** Southwest Autism Research & Resource Center (SARRC) **1C** **D** Ines Shih

2A **D** Tactix Creative **C** self promo—Paul Howalt **2B** **D** Sabingrafik, Inc. **C** Qualcomm **2C** **D** The Drawing Board **C** Gorilla Motor Works

3A **D** Giraffe, Inc. **C** Gorilla Group **3B** **D** Glitschka Studios **C** Pixel Monkey Studios **3C** **D** Glitschka Studios **C** Chinese New Year

4A **D** Glitschka Studios **C** Upper Deck Company **4B** **D** United States of the Art **C** accept & proceed **4C** **D** Jerron Ames **C** Arteis

A

B

C

1

2

3

4

ⒹⒹ = Design Firm   ⒸⒸ = Client

1A Ⓓ Fernandez Design Ⓒ Lincoln Park Zoo 1B Ⓓ Sabingrafik, Inc. Ⓒ San Diego Zoo 1C Ⓓ Leapfrog Marketing Ⓒ Vision Enhanced Studios

2A Ⓓ The Netmen Corp 2B Ⓓ Diagram 2C Ⓓ Infiltrate Media Ⓒ Ape-Love Merchandise 3A Ⓓ A3 Design Ⓒ Dubois County Humane Society

3B Ⓓ Sayles Graphic Design, Inc. Ⓒ Sayles Graphic Design 3C Ⓓ Concepto communication inc. Ⓒ Passion des viandes

4A Ⓓ Roskelly, Inc. Ⓒ Bristol Animal Shelter 4B Ⓓ graphic granola Ⓒ CoolAnimalStuff.com 4C Ⓓ Campbell Fisher Design Ⓒ The Phoenix Zoo

1

2

3

4

D = Design Firm   **C** = Client

1A D Sayles Graphic Design, Inc. **C** maDIKwe **1B D** Kiku Obata & Company **C** St. Louis Zoo **1C D** Siquis **C** Earth Shoes

2A D Sabingrafik, Inc. **C** Helen Woodward Animal Center **2B D** Webster Design Associates, Inc. **C** Henry Doorly Zoo **2C D** Lunar Cow **C** Six Flags Marine World

3A D fuszion **C** Reading Is Fundamental **3B D** Canvas Astronauts & Agriculture **C** The National Zoo—Smithsonian Institute **3C D** VINNA KARTIKA design

4A D GrafiQa Creative Services **C** Paradox Farm **4B D** Boelts Design **C** Zoo Logo **4C D** Heather Boyce-Broddle **C** Pet America

mythology ⊱

A

B

C

1

2

3

4

D = Design Firm   **C** = Client

1A **D** Traction **C** NBA D-League 1B **D** Trapdoor Studio **C** Grupo ñ 1C **D** Traction **C** NBA D-League 2A **D** Gary Sample Design **C** Gary Sample
2B **D** Stiles Design **C** 665 Almost Evil 2C **D** BXC nicelogo.com **C** Discgear.com 3A **D** Richards Brock Miller Mitchell & Associates **C** RBMM—Bowling Team
3B **D** Torch Creative **C** Northwestern State University 3C **D** Clockwork Studios **C** Sixman Football Association
4A **D** Createfirst **C** Available 4B **D** Floor 84 Studio **C** Tom Bellissimo, Special Effects School 4C **D** Sabingrafik, Inc. **C** Hot Rod Hell

D = Design Firm **C** = Client

1A **D** Clockwork Studios **C** San Antonio Diablos FC   1B **D** Storm Design, Inc.   **C** Factory 1969   1C **D** MiresBall **C** Hell Racer

2A **D** Small Dog Design **C** Ballarat Red Devils Soccer Club   2B **D** Sayles Graphic Design, Inc.   **C** Halo Salon   2C **D** CONCEPTiCONS   **C** Yellow Brick Records

3A **D** J.H. van der Heijden   **C** Devils Playground   3B **D** SoupGraphix, Inc.   **C** Bombshell Parts   3C **D** SoupGraphix, Inc.   **C** Bombshell Parts

4A **D** Rubber Cheese   **C** Steam Demons   4B **D** Effusion Creative Solutions   4C **D** Origin Studios   **C** Lucky Devil Studios

1

2

3

4

D = Design Firm **C** = Client

1A **D** LogoDesignSource.com **C** Beacon Blue Demons 1B **D** Patlejch **C** HellPrint
1C **D** Chameleon Design Group, LLC **C** New Jersey Devils, Activate Sport & Entertainment
2A **D** Sebastiany Branding & Design **C** Guia de moteis 2B **D** g79 webdesign **C** g79 webdesign 2C **D** Purplesugar Design **C** Aridsplash Limited
3A **D** SUPERRED **C** Heaven bar 3B **D** Thelogoloft.com **C** Purgatory 3C **D** Richards Brock Miller Mitchell & Associates **C** RBMM—Bowling Team
4A **D** Robert Price **C** Hot Heads 4B **D** Habitat Design **C** Atlanta Demons 4C **D** Formula Design **C** Dragon Monkey Media

Ⓓ = Design Firm   Ⓒ = Client

1A Ⓓ Type Fanatic Design Ⓒ Demon Design   1B Ⓓ 13THFLOOR Ⓒ 20th Century Fox   1C Ⓓ Trapdoor Studio Ⓒ Brimstone

2A Ⓓ volatile-graphics   2B Ⓓ DTM_INC Ⓒ frogbite   2C Ⓓ Casper.Ru Ⓒ CUP

3A Ⓓ Raffaele Primitivo   3B Ⓓ henriquez lara Ⓒ La Diablita Cantina   3C Ⓓ Sayles Graphic Design, Inc. Ⓒ Halo Salon

4A Ⓓ SBE Ⓒ SBE   4B Ⓓ Trapdoor Studio Ⓒ Red Devil Pizzeria   4C Ⓓ MFDI Ⓒ AC Milan, Milanmania.com, Advertency

D = Design Firm   **C** = Client

1A **D** Grindell Design **C** Hacksaw's Garage 1B **D** Sebastiany Branding & Design **C** Guia de Moteis 1C **D** United States of the Art **C** fallen.nl

2A **D** Union Design & Photo **C** Realms of Adventure 2B **D** Reactive Designs **C** Devour Films 2C **D** volatile-graphics

3A **D** ex nihilo **C** Kill my Pain metal band 3B **D** Gyula Nemeth **C** Motiv 3C **D** Stuph Clothing **C** Stuph Clothing

4A **D** Sabingrafik, Inc. **C** Hot Rod Hell 4B **D** United States of the Art **C** superReal 4C **D** Grindell Design **C** Hacksaw's Garage

A

B

C

1

2

3

4

D = Design Firm   **C** = Client

1A **D** Truly Design **C** Truly Design clothing   1B **D** Stuph Clothing **C** Stuph Clothing   1C **D** 13THFLOOR **C** Lincoln Electric

2A **D** Burton (Snowboards) Corp. **C** Burton Snowboards   2B **D** Tim Frame Design **C** touristees.com   2C **D** Scott Oeschger **C** Scott Oeschger

3A **D** Paul Svancara **C** Public Service Announcement   3B **D** Ivey McCoig Creative Partners **C** Dante Cullari   3C **D** Tim Frame Design **C** touristees.com

4A **D** LSD **C** un mundo feliz / a happy world production   4B **D** Device **C** Eagle Imagery **C** (proposal for) Voodoo Surfboards

A   **B**   **C**

1

2

3

4

D = Design Firm   **C** = Client

1A **D** Union Design & Photo   **C** Funnybones   1B **D** Art Chantry   **C** Head Bone   1C **D** Soren Severin   **C** Fictional

2A **D** yarimizoshintaro   2B **D** DZGNBIO   **C** Spootnick.com   2C **D** Stiles+co

3A **D** United States of the Art   **C** tonquelle   3B **D** D&Dre Creative   **C** blackwhite conspiracy   3C **D** D&Dre Creative   **C** blackwhite conspiracy

4A **D** Felixsockwell.com   **C** feluxe   4B **D** R&R Partners   **C** TEP   4C **D** Mike Speero   **C** TrippleDee

Ⓓ = Design Firm   Ⓒ = Client

1A Ⓓ josh higgins design Ⓒ KROQ FM   1B Ⓓ dale harris Ⓒ The Winged   1C Ⓓ Glitschka Studios Ⓒ Upper Deck Company

2A Ⓓ Design Farm Ⓒ Matchbox   2B Ⓓ H2 Design of Texas   2C Ⓓ Tactix Creative

3A Ⓓ Burocratik - Design Ⓒ Cherry Pick   3B Ⓓ thehappycorp global Ⓒ thehappycorp global   3C Ⓓ DUEL Purpose Ⓒ Austin Mopeds

4A Ⓓ United States of the Art Ⓒ superReal   4B Ⓓ Tenacious Design Ⓒ Zipperhead   4C Ⓓ Creative Link Design Ⓒ Old Town Playhouse

1

2

3

4

D = Design Firm C = Client

1A **D** Organi Studios 1B **D** Glitschka Studios **C** Mirra Bikes 1C **D** 13THFLOOR **C** mattel. Inc

2A **D** 13THFLOOR **C** Hot Wheels-Mattel, Inc 2B **D** The Robin Shepherd Group **C** Mr. This 2C **D** MacLean Design **C** Steel Souls

3A **D** Fuze **C** Ghost Cycles 3B **D** 13THFLOOR **C** Hot Wheels-Mattel, Inc 3C **D** 13THFLOOR **C** Hot Wheels-Mattel, Inc

4A **D** creative instinct, inc. **C** X-games athlete 4B **D** Extra Point Creative 4C **D** Clockwork Studios **C** Sixman Football Association

D = Design Firm   **C** = Client

1A **D** harlan creative **C** Brainworks, LLC   1B **D** Respiro Media **C** Carlos Alberto Kunz   1C **D** angryporcupine*design **C** Bumper Sticker

2A **D** BXC nicelogo.com **C** Mattel/13th Floor   2B **D** SoupGraphix, Inc. **C** GordonsWell.com   2C **D** Velocity Design Group **C** Bone Yard Custom Motorcycles

3A **D** Gardner Design **C** Go Away Garage   3B **D** Sayles Graphic Design, Inc. **C** Wild Willy's Cycle Werks   3C **D** reaves design **C** Silly Soft

4A **D** Raffaele Primitivo   4B **D** Storm Design, Inc. **C** Factory 1969   4C **D** Brains on Fire **C** Brains on Fire

1

2

3

4

D = Design Firm   **C** = Client

1A **D** DZGNBIO **C** Peace Off   1B **D** United States of the Art **C** The World Dismay Company   1C **D** Double Brand **C** Skate Shop

2A **D** volatile-graphics   2B **D** Tactix Creative **C** BadDesignKills.com   2C **D** KITA International | Visual Playground **C** fruit

3A **D** SoupGraphix Inc. **C** Excalibur Bail Bonds   3B **D** R&R Partners **C** Harrah's   3C **D** Glitschka Studios **C** Art SOMA—Propaganda III

4A **D** LENOX REIGN **C** Pirate's Paradise   4B **D** Raffaele Primitivo   4C **D** Jolly Dog Ltd **C** Jolly Dog

	A	B	C
1			

D = Design Firm **C** = Client

1A **D** Chris Rooney Illustration/Design **C** Heavenly Ski Resort 1B **D** Scott Oeschger **C** St. Joseph's Preparatory School 1C **D** Valge Vares **C** Parunid & Vonid

2A **D** Stiles Design **C** The Gilbert & Sullivan Society 2B **D** helium.design **C** he2 2C **D** Airtype Studio **C** Skilly Apparel

3A **D** Hubbell Design Works **C** Available 3B **D** 13TH FLOOR **C** Hot Wheels-Mattel, Inc 3C **D** Tower of Babel **C** Davies Motorsports

4A **D** Storm Design, Inc. **C** Factory 1969 4B **D** Haley Johnson Design Co. **C** Qtopia 4C **D** Bryan Cooper Design **C** Hopper's Choppers

A   B   C

1       

2       

3       

4       

D = Design Firm   **C** = Client

1A **D** design june **C** RCA / THOMSON   1B **D** DZGNBIO **C** Spootnick.com   1C **D** THE GENERAL DESIGN CO. **C** National Environmental Trust

2A **D** Glitschka Studios **C** Glitschka Studios   2B **D** United States of the Art **C** usota Shirts   2C **D** Stuph Clothing **C** Stuph Clothing

3A **D** Truly Design **C** Hell dorado   3B **D** Stiles Design **C** Texas Terror   3C **D** Brian Krezel **C** self promo

4A **D** Dr. Alderete **C** NSLM - Max   4B **D** Thielen Designs **C** Militnt Publishing   4C **D** Stiles Design **C** Peace Council

D = Design Firm   **C** = Client

1A **D** Storm Design Inc.   **C** Factory 1969   1B **D** Storm Design, Inc.   **C** Factory 1969   1C **D** J6Studios   **C** Ricochet R & D

2A **D** Liquid Agency   **C** Liquid Agency   2B **D** MiresBall   **C** Chingones   2C **D** DUEL Purpose   **C** Cross Canadian Ragweed

3A **D** www.mieland.de   **C** DevilRiders   3B **D** Kloom   **C** NC Holding, LLC   3C **D** Rocket Science   **C** Airborne Bicycles

4A **D** Carol Gravelle Graphic Design   **C** Golfhead   4B **D** Art Chantry   **C** New Wave Hookers   4C **D** HOOK   **C** Taco Boy

A
B
C

1

2

3

4

D = Design Firm   **C** = Client

1A **D** 13THFLOOR **C** Hot Wheels-Mattel, Inc   1B **D** 13THFLOOR **C** Hot Wheels-Mattel, Inc   1C **D** Hinge **C** Hinge

2A **D** Matt Whitley **C** NWA Roller Girls   2B **D** Stuph Clothing **C** Grits   2C **D** SK+G Advertising **C** Silverton Casino Lodge

3A **D** orton design **C** entityagency.com   3B **D** Floor 84 Studio **C** B&B Effects   3C **D** VIVAMEDIA, Inc. **C** Indianola Record Herald

4A **D** Garcia 360° **C** San Antonio Youth Yes   4B **D** Design Farm **C** Tokyopop   4C **D** laurendesigns **C** For Keeps

Ⓓ = Design Firm   Ⓒ = Client

1A Ⓓ Hinge Ⓒ Hinge   1B Ⓓ 13THFLOOR Ⓒ Hot Wheels-Mattel. Inc   1C Ⓓ 13THFLOOR Ⓒ Hot Wheels-Mattel, Inc

2A Ⓑ SoupGraphix Inc. Ⓒ Adio Footwear   2B Ⓓ Scribblers' Club Ⓒ The Downtown Mudpuppy Chase   2C Ⓓ Timber Design Company Ⓒ Timber Design Co.

3A Ⓓ 13THFLOOR Ⓒ Hot Wheels-Mattel, Inc   3B Ⓓ 13THFLOOR Ⓒ Hot Wheels-Mattel, Inc   3C Ⓓ 13THFLOOR Ⓒ Hot Wheels-Mattel, Inc

4A Ⓓ 13THFLOOR Ⓒ Hot Wheels-Mattel, Inc   4B Ⓓ Gyula Nemeth Ⓒ Budapest Film   4C Ⓓ Sayles Graphic Design, Inc. Ⓒ Road to Ruin Band

	A	B	C
1			
2			
3			
4			

D = Design Firm   **C** = Client

1A **D** STUBBORN SIDEBURN **C** IWYS   **1B** **D** Hinge **C** Hinge   **1C** **D** Formula Design **C** Dragon Monkey Media

2A **D** Art Chantry   **2B** **D** Thielen Designs **C** Hyperactive Music Magazine   **2C** **D** josh higgins design **C** KROQ FM

3A **D** Oxide Design Co. **C** Oxide Design Co.   **3B** **D** FUEL Creative Group **C** Hell Bent Sales   **3C** **D** The Netmen Corp **C** Flaming Angels

4A **D** RDY **C** RDY   **4B** **D** M. Brady Clark Design **C** The Militia Group   **4C** **D** Roskelly Inc. **C** Posh & Naughty

A · B · C

1

2

3

4

D = Design Firm   C = Client

1A **D** Made On Earth **C** 400 Drawings 1B **D** Made On Earth **C** Made On Earth 1C **D** Karl Design Vienna **C** Doris Gassmann

2A **D** Oxide Design Co. **C** Herc Publishing 2B **D** neodesign **C** Taiwan Cheau Wei Co., LTD 2C **D** The Netmen Corp **C** Vital Wellbeing

3A **D** Trifecta Design Group **C** Liberty Wellness & Chiro 3B **D** Ray Dugas Design **C** personal logo 3C **D** bartodell.com **C** Angels

4A **D** Clore Concepts **C** St. John's Clinic 4B **D** Scott Carroll Designs, Inc. **C** Angels on Earth 4C **D** The Russo Group **C** Marriage Enchancement Ministries

1

 Icarus Partners

 **Avascend** Healthcare Hospitality

 **ENGEL-APOTHEKE** Ihre Apotheke am Spital

2

3

 VALLE DE LOS ÁNGELES

 *Gîte* AU LIT DE L'ANGE

4

 RoboSaint

D = Design Firm **C** = Client

1A **D** Jerron Ames **C** Arteis 1B **D** The Collaboration **C** Avascend 1C **D** Kommunikation & Design **C** Engel Apotheke

2A **D** Hand dizajn studio **C** Phoenix Fly, Human Flight Innovations 2B **D** holidayonmars **C** Colt Communication 2C **D** Church Logo Gallery **C** Messenger Resources

3A **D** EXPLORARE **C** Grupo Valle de los Angeles 3B **D** Carmi e Ubertis Milano Srl **C** Angeli 3C **D** Absolu communication marketing **C** Gîte au lit de l'Ange

4A **D** Glitschka Studios **C** Floating Banana, Inc. 4B **D** Extraverage Productions 4C **D** Laura Coe Design Associates **C** La Jolla Playhouse

D = Design Firm   **C** = Client

1A **D** Rubber Cheese **C** Angel Sphere   1B **D** Brian Collins Design **C** Eternal Screenprinting   1C **D** The Logo Factory, Inc.

2A **D** Christian Rothenhagen **C** Berlin Native Clothing   2B **D** www.zka11.com **C** Chio Chips   2C **D** reaves design **C** little angels

3A **D** Morello+Company **C** AT&T   3B **D** BlueSpark Studios **C** Willow Lingerie   3C **D** Carter Design **C** Wish Candles

4A **D** DMG Asociados, S.A. **C** Casa Angel Apartments   4B **D** Diagram **C** IGD Irlandzka Grupa Deweloperska

4C **D** Richard Harrison Bailey/ The Agency **C** Ball State University

D = Design Firm C = Client

Ⓓ = Design Firm   Ⓒ = Client

1A Ⓓ Pinnacle Design Center Ⓒ AquaSpace   1B Ⓓ BT Graphics Ⓒ The Angel Fund   1C Ⓓ Thelogoloft.com Ⓒ Purgatory

2A Ⓓ Gingerbread Lady Ⓒ Glamour Guardian   2B Ⓓ Felixsockwell.com Ⓒ fortune   2C Ⓓ Jonathan Rice & Company Ⓒ Bethesda Community Church

3A Ⓓ moosylvania Ⓒ Halo   3B Ⓓ Ross Hogin Design Ⓒ S.F. Ad Producers   3C Ⓓ Brandoctor Ⓒ MIH   4A Ⓓ co:lab Ⓒ Connecticut Art Directors Club

4B Ⓓ graphic granola Ⓒ Ultra Pure Water   4C Ⓓ Richards Brock Miller Mitchell & Associates Ⓒ Auntie Anne's Pretzel Company

1

2

3

4

D = Design Firm   **C** = Client

1A **D** McQuillen Creative Group **C** Presentation College   1B **D** RADAR Agency **C** Project Read   1C **D** Roskelly Inc. **C** Tori Lynn Andreozzi Foundation

2A **D** Home Grown Logos **C** Home Grown Logos   2B **D** Doug Chatham Design **C** Jan Smith Studios   2C **D** CONCEPTO WORLDWIDE **C** NAKED ANGELS

3A **D** Burocratik - Design **C** Volare Mundia Travel   3B **D** The Drawing Board **C** TAMPA BAY RELOCATION SYSTEMS   3C **D** Hutchinson Associates, Inc. **C** Mercor Media

4A **D** Duffy & Partners **C** St. Paul Travelers   4B **D** Jonathan Rice & Company **C** Pizza Hut   4C **D** Mojo Solo **C** Activ8

A

B

C

1

2

3

4

D = Design Firm   **C** = Client

1A **D** DAVID BARATH DESIGN **C** MTV (Hungarian National TV station)   1B **D** Anoroc **C** Trousdale School   1C **D** Burocratik - Design **C** Volare Mundia

2A **D** CAPSULE **C** Recovery Racing   2B **D** Ulyanov Denis **C** Luxury   2C **D** pricedyment **C** encouraging lives   3A **D** bartodell.com **C** Ares Basketball Apparel

3B **D** Funnel:Eric Kass:Utilitarian+Commercial+Fine:Art **C** Abercrombie & Kent   3C **D** b5 Marketing & Kommunikation GmbH **C** Altima

4A **D** Campbell Fisher Design **C** Champ Car / Vegas Grand Prix   4B **D** Interrobang Design Collaborative, Inc. **C** Big Heavy World   4C **D** volatile-graphics

1

2

3

4

D = Design Firm   **C** = Client

1A **D** TMCA, Inc. **C** PhoenixArtSupply.com   1B **D** Pherra **C** Dannax   1C **D** Extraverage Productions **C** Net Dragon Ltd.

2A **D** Hyperakt **C** Sciascia Electrical Corporation   2B **D** Modern Dog Design Co. **C** K2 Snowboards   2C **D** O'Connor Graphic Design **C** The Write Stuff

3A **D** seesponge **C** DaimlerChrysler   3B **D** cincodemayo **C** Intertrade Motos   3C **D** Bukka Design **C** Last Train Entertainment

4A **D** Kirk Miller **C** Eagle San Diego   4B **D** Erwin-Penland, Inc. **C** Motorola & ScanSource, Inc.   4C **D** c moto **C** Blu Sky Express

{ CULTURE VULTURE }

D = Design Firm   **C** = Client

1A **D** Alarie Design Associates, Inc. **C** Elan Boats   1B **D** Studio Oscar **C** Stussy / Honda   1C **D** Caspari McCormick **C** Delaware Theatre Company

2A **D** Scott Oeschger **C** Saint Joseph's Preparatory School   2B **D** Moss Creative **C** Jetz Americana   2C **D** VanPaul Design **C** dsMedia Inc.

3A **D** A3 Design **C** Griffith Choppers, Inc.   3B **D** Paper Doll Studio **C** Hair 121   3C **D** Dreigestalt **C** Alea Consulting

4A **D** Design Farm **C** Matchbox   4B **D** The Department of Marketing **C** Continuous Blessings Foundation   4C **D** latitude **C** Art Patriot

1

2

3

4

D = Design Firm   **C** = Client

1A **D** Creative United **C** 167   1B **D** Stiles+co **C** Signatures Network   1C **D** McAndrew Kaps **C** McAndrew Kaps

2A **D** Extraverage Productions **C** Logikwear.com   2B **D** Chip Sheean **C** Nine North Wines   2C **D** Citizen

3A **D** Ryan Cooper Design **C** Self Promotion | Marriage   3B **D** Extraverage Productions **C** Personal   3C **D** Sabet Branding **C** Zoobaz Advertising

4A **D** 13THFLOOR **C** Hot Wheels-Mattel, Inc   4B **D** Black Osprey Dead Arts **C** FLIP SKATEBOARDS   4C **D** Tomko Design **C** Shred Lab

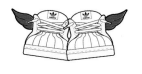

Ⓓ = Design Firm Ⓒ = Client

1A Ⓓ J6Studios Ⓒ TopSite 1B Ⓓ Anoroc Ⓒ Trousdale School 1C Ⓓ Anoroc Ⓒ Trousdale School

2A Ⓓ Pomegranate Studio, Inc. Ⓒ D'Vine Wine 2B Ⓓ 314Creative Ⓒ Résumés From Above 2C Ⓓ R&R Partners Ⓒ Las Vegas Convention & Visitors Authority

3A Ⓓ cypher13 Ⓒ adidas 3B Ⓓ Heather Boyce-Broddle Ⓒ Newman University 3C Ⓓ Gardner Design Ⓒ Ballet Wichita

4A Ⓓ La Visual Ⓒ Sparkle's Angels 4B Ⓓ Gizwiz Studio Ⓒ Abi 4C Ⓓ Bryan Cooper Design Ⓒ AngelFlight

	A	B	C
1			
2			
3			
4			

Ⓓ = Design Firm   Ⓒ = Client

1A Ⓓ PPBH Ⓒ Utah Department of Transportation   1B Ⓓ FUEL Creative Group Ⓒ Rods and Relics Car Club   1C Ⓓ Moss Creative Ⓒ Pacific Headwear

2A Ⓓ Hiebing Ⓒ The Boys & Girls Club of Dane County   2B Ⓓ DesignWorks Group Ⓒ Patterson Dealerships   2C Ⓓ Pump Graphic Ⓒ Pump Graphic

3A Ⓓ R&R Partners Ⓒ Allied Waste   3B Ⓓ artbox studios Ⓒ High Vines   3C Ⓓ Eisenberg and Associates Ⓒ GearUp Express

4A Ⓓ mugur mihai Ⓒ American Rock & Royalty   4B Ⓓ renaud garnier smart rebranding Ⓒ Osborne Design   4C Ⓓ ANS Ⓒ Advanced Neuromodulation Systems, Inc.

KLEMME CONSTRUCTION
Remodeling and Tilesetting

OFFICE ANGELS

PR∆SPERITY PROJECT

FastPack

D = Design Firm   **C** = Client

1A **D** XY ARTS **C** Medtronic Technologies   1B **D** Bryan Cooper Design **C** Klemme Construction   1C **D** Gizwiz Studio **C** The University of Game

2A **D** Karl Design Vienna **C** Karl Design / Marken fuer Morgen   2B **D** D&Dre Creative **C** Office Angels   2C **D** Blockdot, Inc. **C** American Airlines

3A **D** And Partners **C** Joel Diamond Music   3B **D** Copia Creative, Inc. **C** Prasperity   3C **D** Pale Horse Design **C** Zap Skimboards

4A **D** Jon Flaming Design **C** FastPack Couriers   4B **D** Jeff Faught, Faught Design **C** Coca-Cola   4C **D** Burton (Snowboards) Corp. **C** Burton Snowboards

	A	B	C
1			
2			
3			
4			

D = Design Firm **C** = Client

1A **D** UNO **C** San Angel 1B **D** R&R Partners **C** Anderson Dairy 1C **D** Heck Yeah! **C** Taco Mac

2A **D** Insight Design **C** Paraclete Credit Management 2B **D** Boelts Design 2C **D** Carrihan Creative Group **C** Vern's Place

3A **D** J.D. Gordon Advertising **C** RF Mackey 3B **D** The Netmen Corp **C** Monsterhog 3C **D** Jeff Fisher LogoMotives **C** triangle productions!

4A **D** Pense Design **C** Therapy Pets 4B **D** Graves Fowler Creative **C** Yarns International 4C **D** cypher13 **C** Free The Sheep

CENTER FOR ANDEAN FREEDOMS
CENTRO DE LIBERTADES ANDINAS

STRATEGIC
CAPITAL
PARTNERS

IMPRIMERIE

LA RENAISSANCE

VENEZIA
Italian restaurant

VICO EQUENSE®

PRESTIGE
ENTERTAINMENT SERVICES

D = Design Firm   **C** = Client

1A **D** The Branding Box **C** Center of Andean Freedoms   1B **D** Finch Creative **C** Amazon Films   1C **D** Strange Ideas

2A **D** Squires and Company **C** AeroLynx   2B **D** Advertising Intelligence **C** 69FM   2C **D** Eisenberg and Associates **C** DEJ Productions, Inc.

3A **D** Gridwerk **C** Strategic Capital Partners, LLC   3B **D** Parallele gestion de marques **C** La Renaissance printing   3C **D** Jovan Rocanov **C** Venezia Restaurant

4A **D** henriquez lara **C** Vico Equense   4B **D** BenKandoraDESIGN **C** Reaction Design & Printing   4C **D** LCD Incorporated **C** Yung Shin

A

B

C

1

2

3

4

D = Design Firm **C** = Client

1A **D** Davis Design **C** Crestone   1B **D** markatos l moore **D** Disfigure   1C **D** Raffaele Primitivo

2A **D** Chase Design Group **C** Kemper Snowboards   2B **D** StyleStation **C** Finnesand Design   2C **D** Frostgiant design firm **C** Fljotsdalsherad

3A **D** SoupGraphix, Inc. **C** Black Stripe Design   3B **D** Organi Studios   3C **D** pearpod **C** Palm Beach Capital

4A **D** Extraverage Productions **C** Net Dragon Ltd.   4B **D** Liska + Associates Communication Design **D** Douglas Elliman   4C **D** Jeff Fisher LogoMotives **C** Reed College

Comune di **Narni**

Griffin
ENTERTAINMENT

SALAM
STRATEGIC SECURITY SERVICES

BURTON · CUSTOM

St. George's
GRYPHONS

ITACA

GRIFFONS

Shibboleth.

IL CLUB
D'ITALIANO A UCI

D = Design Firm **C** = Client

1A **D** Molly&Partners **C** Comune di Narni 1B **D** APSITS **C** APSITS 1C **D** Visible Ink Design **C** Griffin Entertainment

2A **D** RAMIKILANI **C** Salam 2B **D** Brian Krezel **C** Burton Snowboards 2C **D** Rickabaugh Graphics **C** St. George's High School

3A **D** Canefantasma Studio **C** Pogginbonsi Aredda 3B **D** Muku Studios **C** Muku Studios 3C **D** Clockwork Studios **C** Youth Basketball League of Salt Lake City

4A **D** Chermayeff & Geismar, Inc. **C** Griphon 4B **D** Hinge **C** Internet2 4C **D** 7th Street Design **C** University of California, Irvine

A
B
C

1

HOTEL GREIF

VERY PERSONAL

2

LLOYD
INTERNATIONAL
HONORS COLLEGE

3

4

D = Design Firm   **C** = Client

1A **D** Jeff Ames Creative **C** Scherer Metals, Inc   1B **D** brandStrata **C** Disney   1C **D** Granit **C** Hotel Greif

2A **D** The Netmen Corp **C** Knight Kenwood   2B **D** Mitre Agency **C** Lloyd International Honors College   2C **D** GOLDFINGER c.s. **C** Entertainment

3A **D** Ion Design, Inc. **C** Mineokikaku, Inc.   3B **D** ZEBRA design branding **C** TNPS Corporation   3C **D** M3 Advertising Design **C** Michael Chernine

4A **D** Flaxenfield, Inc. **C** Geämi, Ltd.   4B **D** The Fourth Design **C** Sheedeh Real Estate Group   4C **D** Univisual **C** Messengers

A	B	C

1

2

3

4

D = Design Firm   **C** = Client

1A **D** Brand Anarchy Group **C** Dragon Entertainment   1B **D** Velocity Design Group **C** Golfland Entertainment Services
1C **D** Paragon Marketing Communications **C** Little Dragon   2A **D** Mike Quon/Designation **C** Designation   2B **D** Mike Quon/Designation **C** Designation
2C **D** Shaffer Design Works **C** Dragan Construction   3A **D** Design Farm **C** Tokyopop   3B **D** mad studios **C** DIR marketing consultants
3C **D** Fleishman Hillard **C** Revere Communications   4A **D** Strange Ideas   4B **D** Deep Design **C** UPS   4C **D** FutureBrand **C** Crown Macau

D = Design Firm   **C** = Client

1A **D** Pictogram Studio   **C** Pictogram Studio   1B **D** Raffaele Primitivo   1C **D** Mitre Agency   **C** Su Dragon Yu

2A **D** King Design Office   **C** Mandarin Holdings   2B **D** www.mieland.de   **C** Projektwork for City of Worms   2C **D** Brandbeat   **C** Olympic Council of Asia

3A **D** grow   **C** Ramada Plaza Doha   3B **D** Hai Truong   **C** Kamp Nokturnal   3C **D** Jeff Fisher LogoMotives   **C** UO Chinese Student Association

4A **D** Laura Coe Design Associates   **C** JNR   4B **D** The Robin Shepherd Group   **C** Pale Dragon   4C **D** Alterpop   **C** James Enright Construction

1

2

3

4

D = Design Firm **C** = Client

1A **D** Sean Weber **C** Dolnick Wedding . 1B **D** Parachute Design **C** Sansei, Inc. 1C **D** J6Studios **C** Thomi Hawk

2A **D** Floor 84 Studio **C** Original Productions 2B **D** Fossil **C** Zodiac 2C **D** Farm Design **C** Honda Motorcycle

3A **D** Jerron Ames **C** Arteis 3B **D** 7981design **C** royalparadise 3C **D** Fossil **C** Zodiac 4A **D** Central Connecticut State University **C** fly dragon express service

4B **D** Extraverage Productions **C** Net Dragon Ltd. 4C **D** Gardner Design **C** Dragon Golf Cup Tournament

1

2

3

4

D = Design Firm   **C** = Client

1A **D** Turner Duckworth **C** S.A. Brain & Co, Ltd   1B **D** Extraverage Productions **C** Net Dragon, Ltd.   1C **D** Gardner Design **C** Reno Technology

2A **D** Clockwork Studios **C** Youth Basketball League of Salt Lake City   2B **D** Felixsockwell.com **C** tnn   2C **D** Sound Mind Media

3A **D** Thelogoloft.com **C** Aeromantia   3B **D** Jason Pillon **C** Livermore Valley Charter School   3C **D** Extraverage Productions **C** Net Dragon, Ltd.

4A **D** Monson Media **C** Auto Assets   4B **D** Jeff Faught, Faught Design **C** Charlie Mars Band   4C **D** Karl Design Vienna **C** Doris Gassmann

ⅅ = Design Firm Ⅽ = Client

1A ⅅ XY ARTS Ⅽ Concept 1B ⅅ Thielen Designs Ⅽ Evald Johnson (Standard 17, LLC) 1C ⅅ Glyphica Design Ⅽ Phoenix Bat Company

2A ⅅ MSI Ⅽ The Home Depot 2B ⅅ MSI Ⅽ The Home Depot 2C ⅅ Koester Design Ⅽ Haley Creative

3A ⅅ Zed+Zed+Eye Creative Communications Ⅽ Mere's Fly Spray 3B ⅅ Printt Diseñadores, s.c. Ⅽ Pegaso PCS

3C ⅅ Impressions Design and Print, Ltd Ⅽ Shires Executive Chauffeurs

4A ⅅ Double Brand Ⅽ City of Poznan 4B ⅅ Range Ⅽ City of Dallas 4C ⅅ David Kampa Ⅽ Horsefeathers Trading Company

D = Design Firm **C** = Client

1A **D** DUSTIN PARKER ARTS **C** Noesis Creative 1B **D** Sol Consultores **C** Aeton 1C **D** Sabingrafik, Inc. **C** Steve Miller Band

2A **D** Karl Design Vienna **C** FCB / Spitzner Arzneimittel 2B **D** OPEN **C** Srulik Einhorn 2C **D** Simon & Goetz Design **C** gebrüder schaffrath

3A **D** Brandient **C** ABCompany 3B **D** Jerron Ames **C** Arteis 3C **D** Karl Design Vienna **C** FCB / Spitzner Arzneimittel

4A **D** Diagram **C** Oris Group 4B **D** Jerron Ames **C** Arteis 4C **D** Mklane **C** Impure

ⅅ = Design Firm   **ℂ** = Client

1A ⅅ KITA International I Visual Playground ℂ Darier & Cleef   1B ⅅ freelancer ℂ Bios Design Group   1C ⅅ KITA International I Visual Playground ℂ Darier & Cleef

2A ⅅ Studio IX OPUS ADA ℂ ixopusada   2B ⅅ DTM_INC ℂ HomeBrew Records   2C ⅅ Oluzen ℂ Centauro Security

3A ⅅ Sabingrafik, Inc. ℂ Cranford Group   3B ⅅ Rocketman Creative ℂ Brooklyn Park High School   3C ⅅ Visible Ink Design ℂ Arts Finance

4A ⅅ Double Brand ℂ Tea Light Factory   4B ⅅ tomvasquez.com ℂ Grooming Products for Men   4C ⅅ Double Brand ℂ Hotel Sypniewo

D = Design Firm **C** = Client

1A **D** Diagram **C** ING Real Estate Development   1B **D** Eagle Imagery **C** Centaura   1C **D** POLLARDdesign **C** The Bon Marché

2A **D** Sabingrafik, Inc. **C** Cranford Group   2B **D** Image Now   2C **D** ANS **C** Lake Horse Riding Stables

3A **D** Canyon Creative **C** Caesars Entertainment   3B **D** Sabingrafik, Inc. **C** University of California, San Diego   3C **D** Sabingrafik, Inc. **C** University of California, San Diego

4A **D** Sabingrafik, Inc. **C** Rubios Baja Grill   4B **D** Sabingrafik, Inc. **C** Seafarer Baking Company   4C **D** KW43 BRANDDESIGN **C** Ritzenhoff AG

D = Design Firm   **C** = Client

1A **D** Trapdoor Studio **C** Kingfish 1B **D** Looney Design Lab **C** Kingfish 1C **D** fuszion **C** Atlantis Events

2A **D** Sabingrafik, Inc. **C** University of California, San Diego 2B **D** J6Studios **C** Neptune Surfboards 2C **D** FINAL IMAGE GmbH **C** Neptun Submarines Switzerland

3A **D** Richard Ward Associates **C** Gordon Murray Design Limited 3B **D** Vanderbyl Design **C** Bedford Properties 3C **D** Art Passions Design **C** Creative Components

4A **D** iDgital Design Studio, Inc. **C** Cohen & Co. Creative 4B **D** CF Napa Brand Design **C** Boisset America

4C **D** Coleman Creative Design Studio **C** Mermaid Cottage Rentals

1

2

3

4

D = Design Firm **C** = Client

1A **D** Q Design **C** Piara Jewelry   1B **D** McDougall & Duval Advertising **C** Dan and Bonnie Duval   1C **D** CDI Studios **C** Cabo Esmeralda Resorts

2A **D** Lunabrand Design Group **C** Lunabrand Design Group   2B **D** bob neace graphic design, inc **C** Kelly's   2C **D** helium.design **C** Unitech GmbH

3A **D** Gardner Design **C** Amerimerc   3B **D** The Robin Shepherd Group **C** FLUID Surfboards   3C **D** CONCEPTiCONS **C** Princess Cruises

4A **D** Tactix Creative **C** Boat Locker   4B **D** Capisce Design, Inc. **C** Veronica Malibu   4C **D** Najlon **C** Dsitel & Pristop

D = Design Firm   **C** = Client

1A **D** Natale Design **C** Saturate Entertainment, LLC   1B **D** McGuire Design **C** Claudia Moreno & Robert McGuire   1C **D** Sabingrafik, Inc. **C** The Masters Group

2A **D** CONCEPTiCONS **C** Tropix   2B **D** Sabingrafik, Inc. **C** Cranford Group   2C **D** Banowetz + Company, Inc. **C** The Hamilton Companies

3A **D** Graphic D-Signs, Inc. **C** LightStream Electric   3B **D** Brian Krezel **C** Self Promo   3C **D** Hirschmann Design **C** The Rouse Company

4A **D** San Markos **C** www.siatman.org   4B **D** Clockwork Studios **C** Spin Foundry   4C **D** Felixsockwell.com **C** angelika

	A	B	C
1			
2			
3			
4			

D = Design Firm　**C** = Client

1A **D** Open Creative Group **C** Pixie Dust Gifts　1B **D** Mark Oliver, Inc. **C** Katrina Hanson　1C **D** delphine **C** The Super Dentists

2A **D** Banowetz + Company, Inc. **C** Oz Systems　2B **D** Hubbell Design Works **C** DirecTV Wizard.com　2C **D** Hubbell Design Works **C** The Constellation Group

3A **D** rajasandhu.com　3B **D** Visible Ink Design **C** Ridgeway Dacy　3C **D** Burn Creative **C** Advantica

4A **D** Rickabaugh Graphics **C** University of Central Florida　4B **D** Pro Print Designs **C** Flexshield　4C **D** Absolu communication marketing **C** Solus Sécurité

D = Design Firm   **C** = Client

1A **D** Fitting Group **C** Black Knight Security   1B **D** Zed+Zed+Eye Creative Communications   **C** Vanguard Network Solutions   1C **D** Element   **C** Fairfield Christian Academy

2A **D** Element **C** Worthington Christian Schools   2B **D** Epix **C** Renania   2C **D** Jon Flaming Design **C** The Covenant School

3A **D** XY ARTS **C** ANK Records   3B **D** Iperdesign, Inc. **C** tiberia windows and doors   3C **D** Haven Productions **C** Quixotic Ministries

4A **D** Sabingrafik, Inc. **C** Freelance Productions   4B **D** Sabingrafik, Inc. **C** Valkyrie   4C **D** Sabingrafik, Inc. **C** Valkyrie

[ANGRY ASSOCIATES]

D = Design Firm   **C** = Client

1A **D** Rickabaugh Graphics **C** Seton Hall University   1B **D** Boondock Walker **C** Rocky River High School   1C **D** Glitschka Studios **C** Upper Deck Company

2A **D** Gizwiz Studio **C** Philip   2B **D** Gary Sample Design **C** Neighborhood Developement Association   2C **D** Fine Dog Creative **C** A.G. Edwards

3A **D** Barnstorm Creative Group, Inc **C** Georgtown Raiders Hockey Club   3B **D** United States of the Art **C** CK   3C **D** Brian Krezel **C** Ripcurl

4A **D** Valhalla I Design & Conquer   4B **D** Valhalla I Design & Conquer   4C **D** Valhalla I Design & Conquer

A   B   C

COASTAL
C A F E

TARAHUMARA

1982–2007

1

2

The
Ta'ero
Tiki
Polynesian Lounge

aCE
Tiki

3

SURISOK
A C T I V E   F O O T W E A R

4

D = Design Firm **C = Client**

D = Design Firm **C = Client**

1A **D** Daggerfin **C** Volkswagen Dealer Incentive Trip 1B **D** Farm Design 1C **D** The Robin Shepherd Group **C** The Robin Shepherd Group

2A **D** Velocity Design Group **C** Golfland Entertainment Services 2B **D** RWest **C** OluKai 2C **D** Chip Sheean **C** Unfiltered Napa

3A **D** Squires and Company **C** XTO Energy 3B **D** Tactix Creative **C** Expressions 3C **D** Hinge **C** Hinge

4A **D** Clockwork Studios **C** Sixman Football Association 4B **D** Frostgiant design firm **C** Frostgiant 4C **D** Glitschka Studios **C** Grommie Snowboards

D = Design Firm **C** = Client

1A **D** Advertising Intelligence 1B **D** Shawn Huff **C** Austin Boyd Huff 1C **D** Gramma **C** ThinkRobot
2A **D** Robot Agency Studios **C** Robot Agency Studios 2B **D** Tactix Creative 2C **D** Sayles Graphic Design, Inc. **C** Cedar Rapids Advertising Federation
3A **D** PETTUS CREATIVE **C** Pita Communications: Time Machine 3B **D** Go Media **C** Print Indie 3C **D** Tim Frame Design **C** Ironhead Athletic
4A **D** DUSTIN PARKER ARTS **C** Art Contractor 4B **D** Access Media Lab **C** DJ Savure 4C **D** Storm Design, Inc. **C** Tin Robot

1

PRINT
INDIE

2

3

4

D = Design Firm **C** = Client

1A **D** Ross Hogin Design **C** Upside Events 1B **D** Go Media **C** Print Indie 1C **D** Stiles Design **C** Chad Berry

2A **D** POLLARDdesign **C** Wendy Peyton 2B **D** Alphabet Arm Design **C** Alphabet Arm 2C **D** oakley design studios **C** Osaka Museum of Arts & Sciences

3A **D** Peak Seven **C** The Pugliese Company 3B **D** Velocity Design Group **C** Market Skateboards 3C **D** Sibley Peteet **C** Zilliant

4A **D** Strange Ideas 4B **D** Strange Ideas 4C **D** Gardner Design

Bulwark
Backup

Vzclean

Utility Exploration Center

92.1 FM WTPS
WPTS.ORG

ROBOT
AGENCY
STUDIOS

xcellon
PIXEL PERFECT

METAL
MEN

Banoggle.com

ROCK'EM SOCK'EM
CHAMBER & CVB
2007

TE8AM

D = Design Firm **C** = Client

1A **D** Organi Studios   1B **D** Richard Button Design, LLC **C** Vzclean   1C **D** FUEL Creative Group **C** City of Roseville

2A **D** Fargo Design Co., Inc. **C** University of Pittsburgh   2B **D** Robot Agency Studios   2C **D** Jeff Andrews Design **C** Jeff Andrews

3A **D** Nori Studios **C** Technology Brand   3B **D** KITA International I Visual Playground **C** anti-terror campaign   3C **D** Device

4A **D** Union Design & Photo **C** Banoggle   4B **D** Dustin Commer **C** GWCVB   4C **D** Matt Whitley **C** Wal-Mart

A **B** **C**

1

2

3

4

D = Design Firm   **C** = Client

1A **D** simplegraphics **C** FIC   1B **D** Spoonbend **C** Ticketmotor   1C **D** Gillen's Army **C** Nathan Hanlon

2A **D** cypher13 **C** TEEBEEland   2B **D** cypher13 **C** TEEBEEland   2C **D** cypher13 **C** TEEBEEland

3A **D** Hausch Design Agency LLC **C** Team Spaceman, Lee Schulz, Brookfield, Wisconsin   3B **D** Glitschka Studios **C** Singapore Design

3C **D** Burton (Snowboards) Corp. **C** Burton Snowboards   4A **D** cypher13 **C** TEEBEEland   4B **D** bryon hutchens I graphic design **C** AREA 51 Films

4C **D** Studio Simon **C** Great Falls Voyagers

1

2

3

4

D = Design Firm   **C** = Client

1A **D** X RAY **C** Ufo   1B **D** Logo Orange   1C **D** Burocratik - Design **C** Mediaprimer

2A **D** Octane **C** DJ D6   2B **D** DEVELOPED IMAGE PTE LTD **C** Jelly Pixels.com   2C **D** Hyperakt **C** Disco Lemonade

3A **D** Becky Kent **C** Dwell Development / Proposal   3B **D** VanPaul Design **C** couchmonkey.com   3C **D** BAIRDesign **C** Argonaut Films

4A **D** Glitschka Studios **C** 100 Milligrams   4B **D** Bleutuna Limited **C** Bleutuna Limited   4C **D** Glitschka Studios **C** Upper Deck Company

D = Design Firm **C** = Client

1A **D** Kellum McClain Inc. **C** Unherd of Productions   1B **D** Tactical Magic **C** Lunar Productions   1C **D** Methodikal **C** Methodikal

2A **D** XY ARTS **C** micro gamer   2B **D** volatile-graphics   2C **D** ZupiDesign **C** ZupiHost

3A **D** Advent Creative **C** Creative Communication   3B **D** Hoyne Design   3C **D** dache **C** crackmuffin

4A **D** DZGNBIO **C** Spootnick.com   4B **D** cypher13 **C** cypher13   4C **D** Eli Kirk **C** Utah New Media Conference

D = Design Firm **C** = Client

1A **D** Raffaele Primitivo 1B **D** cypher13 **C** BabyEater 1C **D** Honest Bros. **C** Octopod

2A **D** Dr. Alderete **C** Mostrissimo Records 2B **D** Stiles Design **C** Nice Monster 2C **D** Tactix Creative **C** Tactix

3A **D** Glitschka Studios **C** Street Value 3B **D** LogoMotto.com **C** Alwin Clores—pinoypodcast.com 3C **D** Rain design partners **C** Tara Book Company

4A **D** nGen Works **C** titofelix 4B **D** The Netmen Corp 4C **D** dache **C** nabou

A   B   C

1

2

3

4

Ⓓ = Design Firm   Ⓒ = Client

1A Ⓓ Fuego3 Ⓒ Illego Alien   1B Ⓓ interrabang design studio Ⓒ self promotion   1C Ⓓ Device

2A Ⓓ brandStrata Ⓒ Hero Image Arts   2B Ⓓ Círculodiseño, SC Ⓒ coca cola femsa mexico   2C Ⓓ Origin Studios Ⓒ Jeff Burg DDS

3A Ⓓ Art Chantry Ⓒ Estrus   3B Ⓓ Retro DC Ⓒ Zombie Incorporated   3C Ⓓ Tim Frame Design Ⓒ touristees.com

4A Ⓓ Velocity Design Group Ⓒ self promotion   4B Ⓓ The Netmen Corp Ⓒ Monstermarketing   4C Ⓓ S4LE.com Ⓒ monster ultimate

1

2

3

4

D = Design Firm   **C** = Client

1A **D** M3 Advertising Design **C** Chameleon Studios   1B **D** pearpod **C** learn to ski for good   1C **D** Wox **C** Fulesco S.A.

2A **D** Ray Dugas Design **C** Color Spot Nurseries   2B **D** Whitney Edwards LLC **C** M&M Refrigeration   2C **D** Lunar Cow **C** YMCA Akron

3A **D** reaves design **C** busch gardens   3B **D** V V N Design **C** Bobachine   3C **D** Dotzero Design **C** FrightTown

4A **D** Gizwiz Studio **C** 96khz   4B **D** DTM_INC **C** frogbite   4C **D** Art Chantry **C** Z-Rock Radio

D = Design Firm   **C** = Client

1A **D** Gary Sample Design **C** online contest to design logo   1B **D** Gary Sample Design **C** unused   1C **D** James Good Limited **C** Monster Video

2A **D** Brian Krezel **C** Joy Engine   2B **D** Brian Krezel **C** Joy Engine   2C **D** Gizwiz Studio **C** Morri

3A **D** Hula+Hula **C** Cartoon Network   3B **D** Dotzero Design **C** Bridgetown Printing   3C **D** Device

4A **D** Hula+Hula **C** Fobia   4B **D** Raffaele Primitivo   4C **D** design june **C** cite du design de st etienne

Ⓓ = Design Firm   Ⓒ = Client

1A Ⓓ DZGNBIO Ⓒ dzgnbio   1B Ⓓ United States of the Art Ⓒ tonquelle   1C Ⓓ volatile-graphics

2A Ⓓ Lee Davis Design Ⓒ Ellen Cook Design   2B Ⓓ Jason Kochis Ⓒ Sony Signatures, Inc.   2C Ⓓ S4LE.com Ⓒ Jabberwocky Ultimate

3A Ⓓ Artnak Ⓒ Uros   3B Ⓓ Artnak Ⓒ IK   3C Ⓓ Glitschka Studios Ⓒ Upper Deck Company

4A Ⓓ KHANA SHIRO Ⓒ Appian Way—Leonardo DiCaprio   4B Ⓓ Dr. Alderete Ⓒ Beef   4C Ⓓ Ross Hogin Design Ⓒ Storm Hockey Camps

1

2

ROYAL ARMOURIES MUSEUM

3

THE VISUAL POLLUTION
· ARTIST COOPERATIVE ·

4

D = Design Firm C = Client

1A **D** 343 Creative **C** Hartford Seawolves   1B **D** Alphabet Arm Design **C** Roland Smart / Art Interactive   1C **D** APSITS **C** ST

2A **D** CONCEPTiCONS **C** Vivid Video   2B **D** Minale Tattersfield and Partners Ltd **C** Royal Armouries Museum   2C **D** Glitschka Studios **C** Publisher

3A **D** Studio GT&P   3B **D** DUSTIN PARKER ARTS **C** Proteus Mag   3C **D** DUSTIN PARKER ARTS **C** The Visual Pollution

4A **D** 13THFLOOR **C** 20th Century Fox   4B **D** wray ward **C** jochen tartak   4C **D** Renaud Garnier Smart Rebranding **C** Renaud Garnier Smart Rebranding

A B C

   1

   2

   3

   4

D = Design Firm **C** = Client

1A **D** CONCEPTiCONS **C** Vivid Video 1B **D** CONCEPTiCONS **C** Vivid Video 1C **D** Carmi e Ubertis Milano Srl

2A **D** Moss Creative **C** PolyGram Records 2B **D** Ginter & Miletina 2C **D** Moss Creative **C** PolyGram Records

3A **D** Sarah Grimaldi **C** bambistar clothing 3B **D** R&R Partners 3C **D** Element **C** Columbus Cutters Scooter Club

4A **D** APSITS **C** Space Music 4B **D** DTM_INC **C** frogbite 4C **D** APSITS **C** Latvian National Forests

A

B

C

1

2

3

4

D = Design Firm   **C** = Client

1A **D** Fusion2 Graphics Pty Ltd **C** High Anxiety Team 1B **D** Daniel Matthews **C** Whomp! FM 1C **D** Dirty Design **C** Deep Freaks

2A **D** Studio Simon **C** Trenton Thunder 2B **D** Studio Simon **C** Trenton Thunder 2C **D** Campbell Fisher Design **C** Nirve

3A **D** R&R Partners **C** Nevada Power 3B **D** Strange Ideas **C** Monster Copiers 3C **D** Union Design & Photo **C** Monster Copiers

4A **D** Decoylab **C** Succotash 4B **D** Kjetil Vatne **C** Anagadirri Productions 4C **D** RedBrand **C** 4Mops

index

directory of contributors

01d
Belarus
www.01d.ru
1 Trick Pony
USA
www.1trickpony.com
1310 Studios
USA
www.1310studios.com
13THFLOOR
USA
www.13thfloordesign.com
13thirtyone Design
USA
www.13thirtyone.com
2B Design
USA
724-449-7077
2TREES DESIGN
USA
www.2treesdesignco.com
3 Deuces Design, Inc.
USA
719-232-5411
314creative
USA
770-416-1299
343 Creative
USA
www.343creative.com
360ideas
USA
www.360ideas.com
5 Fifteen Design Group, Inc.
USA
www.5-fifteen.com
7 Lucky Dogs Creative, LLC
USA
www.7luckydogs.com
7981design
China
www.7981design.com
7th Street Design
USA
626-202-4528
903 Creative, LLC
USA
www.903creative.com
9MYLES, Inc.
USA
www.9myles.com
A3 Design
USA
www.athreedesign.com
About350, Inc.
USA
www.about350.com
Absolu communication marketing
Canada
www.absolu.ca
Access Media Lab
USA
301-606-2776
The Action Designer
Norway
www.actiondesigner.com
Ad Impact Advertising
Australia
www.adimpact.com.au
Adams & Knight Advertising & Public Relations
USA
www.adamsknight.com
Adams Design Group
New Zealand
+64 4 971 0182
ADC Global Creativity
USA
www.adc-inc.com
adfinity
USA
www.adfinity.net
Adler & Schmidt Kommunikations-Design
Germany
+49 30 8600070
Advent Creative
USA
www.adventcreative.com

Advertising Intelligence
Kazakhstan
www.artrafael.narod.ru
Advertising Ventures, Inc.
USA
401-453-4748
Airtype Studio
USA
www.airtypestudio.com
AKOFA Creative
USA
www.akofa.com
Alana Jelinek Design
USA
www.alphagrl.com
Alarie Design Associates, Inc.
USA
www.alariedesign.com
Alien Identity
USA
www.alienidentity.com
Alin Golftescu
Romania
+40729937251
alloy studio
Australia
www.alloystudio.com.au
Alphabet Arm Design
USA
www.alphabetarm.com
Altagraf
USA
267-342-3815
Alterpop
USA
415-558-1515
Always Creative
USA
979-446-0578
Amalgamated Studios
USA
818-848-7148
And Partners
USA
www.andpartnersny.com
angryporcupine*design
USA
www.angryporcupine.com
Anoroc
USA
anorocagency.com
ANS
USA
972-526-9642
APSITS
Latvia
www.apsits.com
Aranzamendez Design and Productions
USA
www.aranzamendezdesign.com
Arc Worldwide
Malaysia
www.arcww.com
Archrival
USA
www.archrival.com
Arena Design
USA
www.arenadesign.com
arin fishkin
USA
www.arinfishkin.com
ars graphica
USA
arsgraphica.net
Arsenal Design, Inc.
USA
www.arsenaldesign.com
Art Chantry
USA
253-310-3993
Art Craft Printers & Design
USA
785-776-9151
Art Passions Design
USA
541-322-0909
artbox studios
USA
917-232-9075

ArtGraphics.ru
Russia
www.artgraphics.biz
ARTini BAR
USA
www.artinibar.com
Artnak
Slovenia
www.artnak.net
Artrinsic Design
USA
www.artrinsic.com
asmallpercent
USA
www.asmallpercent.com
Atlantis Visual Graphics
USA
518-541-2093
Atomic Wash Design Studio
USA
www.atomicwash.com
Axiom
USA
713-523-5711
Axiom Design Partners
Australia
www.axiomdp.com.au
b5 Marketing & Kommunikation GmbH
Bergstrasse
www.b5-media.de
baba designs
USA
248-360-1251
Back2Front
Australia
+395840692
BadGenius
USA
www.badgenius.com
BAIRDesign
USA
718-243-1344
Banowetz + Company, Inc.
USA
www.banowetz.com
BarkinSpider Studio
USA
www.barkinspider.com
Barnstorm Creative Group, Inc
Canada
www.barnstormcreative.com
bartodell.com
USA
www.bartodell.com
BDG STUDIO RONIN
USA
240-505-4774
Beacon Branding, LLC
USA
www.beaconbranding.com
Becky Kent
USA
612-703-6315
BenKandoraDESIGN
USA
www.benkandoradesign.com
Bertz Design Group
USA
www.bertzdesign.com
Beth Singer Design
USA
www.bethsingerdesign.com
Beveridge Seay, Inc.
USA
www.bevseay.com
Big Communications
USA
www.bigcom.com
Black Barn Brand Design
USA
blackbarnsc.com
Black Crow Studio
USA
www.blackcrowstudio.com
Black Osprey Dead Arts
USA
Blake BW
Argentina
www.blakebw.com

BLAM, Inc.
USA
785-979-6799
BlaseDesign
USA
www.blasedesign.com
Blattner Brunner
USA
www.blattnerbrunner.com
Bleutuna Limited
USA
www.qmanning.com/design
Blockdot, Inc.
USA
www.blockdot.com
Blue Bee Design
USA
bluebdesign.com
Blue Clover
USA
www.blueclover.com
Blue Sky Design, Inc.
USA
Blue Storm Design
New Zealand
+64 4 562 8771
Blue Studios, Inc.
USA
www.bluestudios.com
Blue Tomato Graphics
USA
www.bluetomatographics.com
Blue Tricycle, Inc.
USA
www.bluetricycle.com
Bluespace Creative, Inc.
USA
www.bluespacecreative.com
BlueSpark Studios
USA
310-394-9080
bob neace graphic design, inc
USA
316-264-4952
Boelts Design
USA
www.boeltsdesign.com
Bonilla Design
USA
847-791-3491
Boondock Walker
USA
www.boondockwalker.com
Born to Design
USA
www.born-to-design.com
Bounce Design Newcastle Pty, Ltd
Australia
+61 2 4969 3334
BPG Design
Arab Emirates
97142953456
The Bradford Lawton Design Group
USA
www.bradfordlawton.com
Bradshaw Design
Canada
www.bradshawdesign.ca
BrainBox Studio
Israel
+972 4 9907 933
Brains on Fire
USA
www.brainsonfire.com
Brand Anarchy Group
USA
www.brandanarchygroup.com
Brand Engine
USA
www.brandengine.com
Brandbeat
United Arab Emirates
97143216615
BrandBerry
Russia
www.brand-berry.ru
BrandExtract
USA
713-942-7959

Brandient
Romania
www.brandient.com
The Branding Box
USA
804-355-4645
The BrandingHouse
USA
www.thebrandinghouse.com
BrandLogic
USA
www.brandlogic.com
Brandoctor
Croatia
00385 99 2117 507
BRANDSTORM CREATIVE GROUP
USA
305-960-2038
brandStrata
USA
www.brandstrata.com
Braue: Brand Design Experts
Germany
www.braue.info
Brian Blankenship
USA
www.brianblankenship.com
Brian Collins Design
USA
Brian Krezel
USA
www.briankrezel.com
Brickhouse Creative
USA
406-586-3871
Bright Strategic Design
USA
www.brightdesign.com
Brook Group, LTD
USA
www.brookgroup.com/branding
Brown Ink Design
Australia
www.brownink.com.au
Bryan Cooper Design
USA
www.cooperillustration.com
bryon hutchens | graphic design
USA
310-621-0677
BT Graphics
USA
513-777-8816
Built Creative
USA
919-567-3342
Bukka Design
USA
www.bukkadesign.com
Bulldog & Braun
USA
816-872-4055
Burd & Patterson
USA
www.burdandpatterson.com
Burn Creative
USA
www.burncreative.com
Burocratik - Design
Portugal
www.burocratik.com
Burton (Snowboards) Corp.
USA
802-652-3777
BXC nicelogo.com
USA
www.nicelogo.com
Bystrom Design
USA
www.bystromdesign.com
c moto
USA
www.c-moto.com
c3
USA
913-327-2241
Cabbage Design Company
USA
415-285-0154

Cacao Design
Italy
www.cacaodesign.it

Calacampania Studios
USA
www.ronaldjcala2.com

CaliCat Design & Web Consulting
USA
www.calicatdesign.com

Campbell Fisher Design
USA
www.thinkcfd.com

Candor Advertising
USA
www.candorad.com

Canefantasma Studio
Italy
www.canefantasma.com

Canvas Astronauts & Agriculture
USA
www.bethecanvas.com

canvas design consultants
Australia
02 9281 4438

Canyon Creative
USA
702-262-9901

Canyon Creative
USA
www.canyoncreative.com

Capisce Design, Inc.
USA
310-216-7042

Cappelli Communication srl
Italy
www.ccommunication.it

CAPSULE
USA
www.capsule.us

Carmi e Ubertis Milano Srl
Italy
www.communicationdesign.it

Carol Gravelle Graphic Design
USA
www.carolgravelledesign.com

Carrihan Creative Group
USA
www.carrihan.com

Carter Design
USA
323-384-5629

Caspari McCormick
USA
www.casparimccormick.com

Casper.Ru
Russia
www.portfolio.casper.ru/eng

Casscles Design, Inc
USA
www.cassclesdesign.com

Catalyst Logo Design
USA
www.catalystlogos.com

cc design
USA
423-979-3151

CD Austin
USA
512-947-5934

CDI Studios
USA
www.cdistudios.com

Central Connecticut State University
USA
860-832-0074

CF Napa Brand Design
USA
www.cfnapa.com

Chameleon Design Group, LLC
USA
www.chameleondg.com

Chanpion Design
Australia
0423 56 56 65

Charles Akins_AkinsTudio
USA
www.akinstudio.com

Charles Design
USA
www.charlesdesigninc.com

Chase Design Group
USA
www.margochase.com

Checkerberry Graphics, Inc.
USA
www.checkerberrygraphics.com

Chermayeff & Geismar, Inc.
USA
www.cgstudionyc.com

Chimera Design
Australia
www.chimera.com.au

Chip Sheean
USA
707-225-4164

Chris Malven Design
USA
www.chrismalven.com

Chris McCampbell
USA
619-865-3124

Chris Rooney Illustration/Design
USA
www.looneyrooney.com

Christian Rothenhagen
Germany
www.christianrothenhagen.com

Christine Case Design
USA
www.christinecasedesign.com

Church Art Works
USA
www.churchartworks.com

Church Logo Gallery
USA
www.churchlogogallery.com

cincodemayo
Mexico
www.cincodemayo.com.mx

Círculodiseño, SC
Mexico
www.circulodiseno.com.mx

Cirque de Darmon
USA
402-202-9119

Cisneros Design
USA
505-471-6699

Citizen
USA
www.wearecitizen.com

clicketyclick
UK
+44(0)1666 860 584

Clockwork Studios
USA
210-545-3415 ext. 107

Clore Concepts
USA
417-881-1722

Clover Creative Group, LLC
USA
www.clovercreativegroup.com

Clutch Design
USA
www.clutchla.com

co.lab
USA
www.colabinc.com

Cocoon
Canada
www.cocoonbranding.com

Coleman Creative Design Studio
USA
843-476-6537

Colin Saito
USA
www.colinsaito.com

The Collaboration
USA
www.the-collaboration.com

Collaboration Reverberation
USA
www.thecrstudio.com

Colorblind Chameleon
USA
www.colorblindchameleon.com

Combustion
USA
www.thesparkmachine.com

Communication Arts
USA
www.commarts-boulder.com

Compass Design
USA
www.compassdesigninc.com

CONCEPTiCONS
USA
www.concepticons.net

Concepto communication, inc.
Canada
www.conceptoinc.qc.ca

CONCEPTO WORLDWIDE
Dominican Republic
809-965-6592

concussion, llc
USA
817-336-6824 ext. 207

Conover
USA
www.studioconover.com

Cooper Design
USA
512-989-8497

Copia Creative, Inc.
USA
www.copiacreative.com

Courtney & Company
USA
www.courtneyco.com

Crain Associates
USA
www.crainassociates.com

CRE8 design co.
USA
651-253-2724

Createfirst
USA
www.createfirst.com

Creative Beard
USA
www.creativebeard.com

Creative Impact, Inc.
USA
creativeimpactgraphics.com

creative instinct, inc.
USA
www.creativeinstinct.com

Creative Link Design
USA
312-848-9453

Creative Madhouse
USA
www.creativemadhouse.com

Creative NRG
USA
www.creative-nrg.com

Creative United
Australia
www.creativeunited.com.au

Cuie&Co
South Africa
www.cuieandco.com

Culp Design
USA
www.culpdesign.com

Culture A.D.
USA
www.culture-ad.com

Culture Pilot
USA
713-868-4100

CVAD_CommunicationDesign
USA
940-565-4287

cypher13
USA
www.cypher13.com

D&Dre Creative
USA
www.deandrecreative.com

D&i (Design and Image)
USA
www.seebrandgo.com

dache
Switzerland
www.dache.ch

Daggerfin
USA
www.daggerfin.com

DAGSVERK - Design and Advertising
Iceland
www.dagsverk.is

Dale Harris
Australia
www.daleharris.com

dandy idea
USA
www.dandyidea.com

Daniel Matthews
UK
www.danielmatthews.net

Daniel Scharfman Design, Inc.
USA
212-941-6277

Daniel Sim Design
Australia
www.danielsim.com/landing.html

David & Associates
USA
402-462-6226

DAVID BARATH DESIGN
Hungary
www.davidbarath.com

David Barron
USA

David Clark Design
USA
www.davidclarkdesign.com

David Gramblin
USA
918-261-2042

David Kampa
USA
512-636-3791

David Maloney
USA
www.david-maloney.com

David Meyer Studio
USA
www.davidmeyerstudio.com

David Russell Design
USA
www.davidrusselldesign.com

Davidson Branding
Australia
www.davidsonbranding.com

Davis Design
USA
303-399-8111

davpunk!
USA
www.davpunk.com

Decoylab
USA
www.decoylab.com

Deep Design
USA
deepdesign.com

Delikatessen
Germany
www.delikatessen-hamburg.com

delphine
USA
858-759-7181

Demographic, Inc.
USA
www.demographicinc.com

DEMOLID Inc.
Hungary
www.demolid.hu

Denis Olenik Design Studio
Belarus
www.denisolenik.com

Dennard, Lacey & Associates
USA
www.dennardlacey.com

The Department of Marketing
USA
919-256-3793

Design Coup, Inc.
USA
404-378-9029

Design Farm
USA
310-266-5921

Design Hovie Studios, Inc.
USA
hovie.com

Design Invasion
USA
314-646-7673

design june
France
www.designjune.com

Design Matters Inc!
USA
www.designmattersinc.com

Design Outpost
USA
www.designoutpost.com

the design spring
USA
773-318-9097

designheavy
USA
www.designheavy.com

Designland
Australia
www.designland.com.au

DesignLingo
USA
www.designlingo.com

DesignPoint, Inc.
USA
www.designpointinc.com

DesignWorks Group
USA
940-696-1229

DEVELOPED IMAGE PTE LTD
Singapore
65 97862302

Device
UK
www.devicefonts.co.uk

Diagram
Poland
www.diagram.pl

Diana Graham
Germany
-102233

die Transformer
Germany
www.die-transformer.de

Digital Flannel
USA
digitalflannel.com

Digital Slant
USA
www.digitalslant.com

Dino Design
USA
www.dinodesign-o.com

Dirty Design
UK
www.dirtydesign.co.uk

Ditto!
USA
www.DittoDoesIt.com

dk design
USA
818-763-9448

DMG Asociados, S.A.
Panama
-1488

Dogstar
USA
www.dogstardesign.com

Doink, Inc.
USA
www.doinkdesign.com

DONATELLI+ASSOCIATES
USA
www.donatelliassociates.com

Dotzero Design
USA
www.dotzerodesign.com

Double Brand
Poland
www.doublebrand.pl

Doug Chatham Design
USA
www.dougchatham.com

Douglas Beatty
UK
+44 079 603 007 12

Dr. Alderete
Mexico
www.jorgealderete.com

Dragyn Studios
USA
www.dragynstudios.com

Draplin Design Co.
USA
www.draplin.com

The Drawing Board
USA
www.tdbgraphics.com

Dreigestalt
Germany
www.dreigestalt.com

DTM_INC
Netherlands
075 635 52 46

DUEL Purpose
USA
www.duelpurpose.com

Duffy & Partners
USA
www.duffy.com

Dustin Commer
USA
www.dustincommer.com

DUSTIN PARKER ARTS
USA
www.dustinparkerarts.com

Dylan Menges
USA
www.dylanmenges.com

DZGNBIO
France
www.dzgnbio.com

E. Tage Larsen Design
USA
917-881-2863

Eagle Imagery
UK
www.eagleimagery.co.uk

e-alw.com
Poland
www.e-alw.com

edesign
USA
301-564-6699

Effective Media Solutions
Canada
www.thinkeffective.com

Effusion Creative Solutions
USA
www.effusiondesign.com

eggnerd
USA
www.eggnerd.com

Eggra
Macedonia
www.eggra.com

eight a.m. brand design (shanghai) Co., Ltd
China
www.8-a-m.com

eindruck design
USA
www.eindruckdesign.com

Eisenberg and Associates
USA
www.eisenberg-inc.com

El Paso, Galeria de Comunicacion
Spain
www.elpasocomunicacion.com

Element
USA
www.elementville.com

Elevata
USA
www.elevatainc.com

Elevation Creative Studios
USA
www.elevationcreative.com

eleven07
USA
347-683-8414

Eli Atkins Design
USA
www.fightthecomputer.com

Eli Kirk
USA
801-377-9321

ellen bruss design
USA
www.ebd.com

Elumin Creative Agency
USA
www.elumin.com

Embryo Design
Norway
www.embryo.no

EMC illustration & design
USA
www.rubricator.net

Endura
USA
501-217-9191

Emerge Design Group
USA
www.emergedesigngroup.com

Enforme Interactive
USA
www.8vodesigns.com

Entermotion Design Studio
USA
www.entermotion.com

Entropy Brands
USA
www.entropybrands.com

Epix
Romania
www.epix.ro

Eric Medalle Design
USA
206-329-2805

Erwin-Penland, Inc.
USA
www.erwinpenland.com

Eskil Ohlsson Assoc. Inc.
USA
252-638-2779

Esparza Advertising
USA
505-765-1505

Estudio Ray
USA
www.estudioray.com

Evenson Design Group
USA
evensondesign.com

ex nihilo
Belgium
www.exnihilo.be

Exhibit A: Design Group
Canada
604-873-1583

EXPLORARE
Mexico
www.explorare.com

Extra Point Creative
USA
www.extrapointcreative.com

Extraverage Productions
Hungary
www.extraverage.net

Ezzo Design
Portugal
+351 229969263

Fandam Studio
South Africa
+27(0)829017699

Fargo Design Co., Inc.
USA
www.fargodesignco.com

Farm Design
USA
www.farmdesign.net

faucethead creative
USA
www.faucethead.com

FDTdesign
USA
www.fdtdesign.com

Federico Rozo
USA
786-260-4244

Felixsockwell.com
USA
www.felixsockwell.com

Fernandez Design
USA
www.fernandezdesign.com

FINAL IMAGE GmbH
Germany
www.final-image.de

Finch Creative
USA
www.finchcreative.com

Fine Dog Creative
USA
www.finedogcreative.com

Fire Monkey Design Studio
Canada
306-692-5142

FIRON
Russia
www.firon.com

First Net Impressions, LLC
USA
www.firstnetimpressions.com

Fitting Group
USA
www.fittinggroup.com

Flaxenfield, Inc.
USA
www.flaxenfield.com

Fleishman Hillard
USA
314-982-9149

Floor 84 Studio
USA
818-754-1231

The Flores Shop
USA
www.thefloresshop.com

Flying Chicken Studios
USA
www.art.mychickenart.com

Fons Schiedon
The Netherlands
www.fonztv.nl

Formula Design
USA
www.formuladesign.com

Fossil
USA
972-699-4923

The Fourth Design
USA
425-268-9687

Fox Fire Creative
USA
www.foxfirecreative.com

Fredrik Lewander
Sweden
www.portfolios.com/fredrik-lewander

FREEHALL. Diseño & Ilustración
Mexico
www.freehall.com.mx

freelancer
Russia
www.flickr.com/photos/bubbo-tubbo

Fresh Oil
USA
www.freshoil.com

Freshwater Design
USA
www.rhondafreshwater.com

Friends University
USA
www.friends.edu

Frostgiant design firm
USA
www.frostgiant.net

Fuego3
USA
www.fuego3.com

FUEL Creative Group
USA
916-669-1591

Fuelhaus Brand Strategy + Design
USA
www.fuelhaus.com

Fumiko Noon
USA
619-261-7118

Funk/Levis & Associates, Inc.
USA
www.funklevis.com

Funnel Design Group
USA
www.funneldesigngroup.com

Funnel:Eric Kass:Utilitarian +Commercial+Fine:Art
USA
www.funnel.tv

Fusion2 Graphics Pty Ltd
Australia
www.fusion2graphics.com.au

fuszion
USA
www.fuszion.com

futska llc
USA
www.futska.com

FutureBrand
Australia
www.futurebrand.com.au

Fuze
USA
www.ifuze.com

Fuzzy Duck Design
USA
www.fuzzyduck.com

g79 webdesign
Hungary
+36 20 578 1484

Gabi Toth
Romania
www.toth.ro

Gable Design Group
USA
www.gable206.com

Gábor Lakatos
Hungary
+36 20 957 0646

Galperin Design, Inc.
USA
www.galperindesign.com

Garcia 360°
USA
210-222-1591

Gardner Design
USA
316-691-8808
www.gardnerdesign.com

Garfinkel Design
USA
www.garfinkeldesign.com

Gary Sample Design
USA
513-271-7785

Garza-Allen Designs
USA
281-804-9436

Gateway Communications
USA
503-257-0100

GCG
USA
817-332-4600

Gee + Chung Design
USA
www.geechungdesign.com

Gee Creative
USA
843-853-4086

THE GENERAL DESIGN CO.
USA
www.generaldesignco.com

Genesis Creative
USA
www.gencreative.com

Geneva Marketing Group
USA
724-430-9844

Gerard Huerta Design
USA
www.gerardhuerta.com

Ted Gibbs at Titanium Design
USA
773-206-6054

Gibson
UK
www.thisisgibson.com

Giles Design, Inc.
USA
210-224-8378

Gillen's Army
USA
www.gillensarmy.com

ginger griffin marketing and design
USA
www.wehaveideas.com

GingerBee Creative
USA
406-443-3032

Gingerbread Lady
UK
www.gingerbread-lady.co.uk

Ginter & Miletina
Germany
www.ginter-miletina.de

Giorgio Davanzo Design
USA
206-328-5031

Giraffe, Inc.
USA
www.giraffesite.com

Gizwiz Studio
Malaysia
www.logodesigncreation.com

Glitschka Studios
USA
www.glitschka.com

Glyphica Design
USA
614-406-9240

GMMB
USA
202-572-2805

Go Graphic
Lebanon
www.gographicdesign.com

Go Media
USA
216-939-0000

Go Welsh
USA
www.gowelsh.com

gocreativ
USA
301-331-3614

GodwinGroup
USA
601-360-9433

GOLDFINGER c.s.
USA
www.goldfingercreative.com

Grafıkona, design studio
USA
505-238-7153

GrafiQa Creative Services
USA
www.grafiqa.com

Gramma
Belgium
www.gramma.be

Granit
Italy
www.granitweb.it

Grant Currie
Canada
www.calderbateman.com

Grapefruit
Romania
www.grapefruit.ro

Graphic Communication Concepts
India
+ 91 22 2284 0206

Graphic D-Signs, Inc.
USA
www.graphicd-signs.com

graphic granola
USA
512-326-3690

Graphic Moxie, Inc.
USA
910-256.8990

Graphic-FX
USA
865-983-0363

Graphismo
USA
www.graphismo.com

Graves Fowler Creative
USA
www.gravesfowler.com

Green Bird Media
USA
619-291-5303

Green Dog Studio
USA
404-788-8053

Green Ink Studio
USA
www.greeninkstudio.com

Greteman Group
USA
gretemangroup.com

Grey Matter Group
USA
www.greymattergroup.com

Gridwerk
USA
www.gridwerk.net

Grindell Design
USA
www.grindelldesign.com

Ground Zero Communications
USA
954-509-1075

grow
Qatar
www.growqatar.com

Grow Design
USA
401-635-8635

Grunt Advertising^Design
USA
www.gruntgraphics.com

Guard Dog Brand Development
USA
212-529-0291

Guernsey Graphics
USA
207-829-4023

Gyula Nemeth
Hungary
www.seadevilworks.blogspot.com

H2 Design of Texas
USA
www.h2dot.com

Habitat Design
USA
www.designbyhabitat.com

Hai Truong
Australia
www.hai.com.au

Haley Johnson Design Co.
USA
www.hjd.com

Haller Design
USA
480-390-8722

Hammerquist & Nebeker
USA
425-285-3362

Hand dizajn studio
Croatia
www.hand.hr

Harbinger
USA
919-232-5080

harlan creative
714-469-0795

Hausch Design Agency LLC
USA
www.hauschdesign.com

Haven Productions
USA
www.havenproductions.net

Hayes+Company
Canada
416-536-5438

Heather Boyce-Broddle
USA
316-744-6267

hecht design
USA
www.hechtdesign.com

Heck Yeah!
USA
www.heckyeah.com

Heisel Design
USA
www.heiseldesign.com

Helium Creative, Inc.
USA
www.heliumcreative.com
helium.design
Germany
www.heliumdesign.de

Helius Creative Advertising
USA
www.freewebs.com/utahrugbyguy/index.htm

Helix Design Communications
Canada
780-413-1822

HendrixRaderWise
USA
317-251-4332

henriquez lara
Mexico
www.henriquezlara.com

Hep
Turkey
www.hep.com.tr

Hexanine
USA
www.hexanine.com

Hiebing
USA
www.hiebing.com

High Fiber Design
Switzerland
www.highfiberdesign.com

Hill Aevium
USA
www.hillaevium.com

Hill Design Studios
USA
www.hilldesignstudios.com

Hinge Incorporated
USA
www.pivotalbrands.com

Hip Street
USA
www.hipst.com

Hirschmann Design
USA
303-449-7363

Hirshorn Zuckerman
Design Group
USA
www.hzdg.com

HMK Archive
USA
www.hmktest.blogspot.com

holidayonmars
Germany
+4.940412627e+011

HollanderDesignLab
USA
www.erikart.com

Home Grown Logos
USA
www.homegrownlogos.com

Honest Bros.
USA
303-847-8225

Honey Design
Canada
www.honey.on.ca

HOOK
USA
www.hookusa.com

Hornall Anderson
USA
www.hadw.com

Hot Dog Design
USA
217-528-3826

Hotiron Creative, LLC
USA
www.hotironcreative.com

Houston &
USA
www.houstonand.com

Howerton+White
USA
www.howertonwhite.com

Howling Good Designs
USA
www.howlinggooddesigns.com

Hoyne Design
Australia
www.hoyne.com.au

Hubbell Design Works
USA
www.hubbelldesignworks.com

HuebnerPetersen
USA
970-663-9344

Hula+Hula
Mexico
www.hulahula.com.mx

Hutchinson Associates, Inc.
USA
www.hutchinson.com

Hutchinson Associates, Inc.
USA
hutchinson.com

Hyperakt
USA
www.hyperakt.com

I Design Creative Group
USA
www.idcreativegroup.com

Idea Girl Design
USA
310-623-2288

identity studios
USA
678-793-4491

iDigital Design Studio, Inc.
USA
954-701-8913

IE Design + Communications
USA
310-376-9600

Illustra Graphics
USA
www.illustra-graphics.com

I'm Design
Portugal
www.behance.net/hugraphic/frame

The Image Designers Group
USA
305-858-1420

The Image Group
USA
www.imagegroup.com

Image Now
Ireland
www.imagenow.com

Imaginaria
USA
www.imaginariacreative.com

Impressions Design and
Print Ltd
UK
www.impressionsdesignandprint.co.uk

Incitrio
USA
619-542-0058

Indicia Design, Inc
USA
www.indiciadesign.com

Ines Shih
USA
650-740-6178

Infiltrate Media
South Africa
www.infiltratemedia.co.za

Ink Graphix
Sweden
www.inkgraphix.com

innfusion studios
USA
www.innfusionstudios.com

Insight Design
USA

interrabang design studio
USA
www.interrabang.com

Interrobang Design
Collaborative, Inc.
USA
www.interrobangdesign.com

Ion Design Inc.
Canada
www.iondesign.ca

Iperdesign, Inc.
USA
www.iperdesign.com

Iskender Asanaliev
Turkey
www.behance.net/iskender

Ivan Manolov
Bulgaria
www.behance.net/Adder

Ivey McCoig Creative Partners
USA
www.iveymccoig.com

J.D. Gordon Advertising
USA
www.jdgordonadvertising.com

J.H. van der Heijden
Netherlands
www.jhvanderheijden.nl

J.Williams Design
USA
616-949-5924

J6Studios
USA
www.j6studios.com

Jackrabbit Design
USA
www.jumpingjackrabbit.com

Jacq Design, LLC
USA
www.jacqdesign.com

Jakob Maser Design
Germany
www.jakobmaser.com

James Good Limited
UK
www.jamesgood.co.uk

James Olson Design
USA
612-618-3159

Jamie Homer
UK
www.circleof10.co.uk

Jane M Illustration
USA
www.janemjolsness.com

Janet Allinger
USA
www.janetallinger.com

Jason Drumheller
USA
www.jasondrumheller.com

Jason Kochis
USA
www.jasonkochis.com

Jason Pillon
USA
925-243-1936

Jean Peterson Design
USA
301-631-2401

Jeff Ames Creative
USA
www.jacreative.org

Jeff Andrews Design
USA
www.jeffandrewsdesign.com

Jeff Faught, Faught Design
USA
www.faughtdesign.com

Jeff Fisher LogoMotives
USA
www.jfisherlogomotives.com

Jeff Kern Design
USA
www.jeffkerndesign.com

Jenn David Design
USA
www.jenndavid.com

Jennifer Braham Design
USA
512-707-9023

Jeremy Stott
USA
801-334-5499

Jerron Ames
USA
801-636-7929

JG Creative
USA
www.jgc.me

Jill Carson Design
USA
www.jillcarson.com

Jill Steinfeld : Design Studio
USA
415-931-2689

JM Design Co.
USA
www.jmdesignco.net

Jobi
Arab Emirates
9.7150494368e+011

The Joe Bosack Graphic
Design Co.
USA
www.joebosack.com

John Silver
USA
www.johnsilveronline.com

Jolly Dog Ltd
Virgin Islands
www.thejollydog.com

Jon Flaming Design
USA
www.jonflaming.com

Jonathan Rice & Company
USA
www.jriceco.com

Jones Design
USA
www.gregorybjones.com

joni dunbar design
USA
601-520-3309

Joseph Blalock
USA
www.josephblalock.com

josh higgins design
USA
www.joshhiggins.com

Jovan Rocanov
Serbia
www.rocanov.com

Juancazu
Colombia
313 350 4044

Judson Design
USA
www.judsondesign.com

Juice Media
USA
www.juicemultimedia.com

Juicebox Designs
USA
615-297-1682

julian peck
USA
415-246-4897

JumpDog Studio
USA
www.jumpdogstudio.com

Just2Creative
USA
www.just2creative.com

Kahn Design
USA
www.kahn-design.com

Kane and Associates
UK
www.kaneandassociates.co.uk

Kari Piippo Oy
Finland
www.piippo.com/kari

Karl Design Vienna
Austria
www.karl-design-logos.com

Karmalaundry
USA
www.karmalaundry.com

Kastelov
Bulgaria
www.kastelov.com

Kat & Mouse Graphic Design
USA
414-961-1593

Kellum McClain, Inc.
USA
www.kellummcclain.com

KENNETH DISENO
Mexico
www.kengraf.net

Kevin Creative
Canada
www.kevincreative.com

Keyword Design
USA
www.keyworddesign.com

KHANA SHIRO
USA
www.khanashiro.com

Kiku Obata & Company
USA
www.kikuobata.com

Killustration, Ink.
USA
www.killustrationink.com

Kindred Design Studio, Inc.
USA
www.kindredesign.com

Kinesis, Inc.
USA
www.kinesisinc.com

Kineto
Indonesia
+61-21 8317118

King Design Office
USA
www.kingdesignoffice.com

Kingston Partners
USA

Kirk Miller
USA
www.KirkMiller.us

KITA International | Visual
Playground
Germany
www.kita-berlin.com

Kitemath
USA
www.kitemath.com

Kjetil Vatne
Norway
www.kvad.com

Kloom
Brazil
+55 (11) 3884-0549

KNOCKinc.
USA
612-333-6511

The Know
Australia
+61 395337662

Kobalto
Spain
www.kobalto.com

Koester Design
USA
www.koesterdesign.com

Koetter Design
USA
502-515-3092

Kommunikation & Design
Germany
www.kommunikation-design.de

Koodoz Design
Australia
www.koodoz.com.au

Kradel Design
USA
610-505-0121

Kraftaverk - Design Studio
Iceland
www.kraftaverk.is

KRE8IVE design
USA
www.kre8ive.net

Kreatory Studio
Australia
www.kreatory.com.au

KTD
USA
www.ktd.com

Kurt for Hire
USA
www.kurtforhire.com

Kurt Snider Design
USA
702-767-1536

KW43 BRANDDESIGN
Germany
www.kw43.de

Kym Abrams Design
USA
www.kad.com

L*U*K*E
USA
612-342-9701

La Visual
USA
www.lavisual.com

Landor Associates
USA
www.sfo.landor.com

Langton Cherubino Group
USA
212-533-2585

The Laster Group
USA
www.lastergroup.com

latitude
USA
214-696-7906

Laura Coe Design Associates
USA
619-223-0909

Laurel Black Design, Inc.
USA
www.laurelblack.com

laurendesigns
USA
www.laurendesigns.com

LCD Incorporated
USA
415-902-5642

Leah Hartley
Australia
www.leahhartley.com

Leapfrog Marketing
USA
www.leapfrogmktg.com

LeBoYe
Indonesia
+62 21 7199676

Lee Davis Design
USA
423-488-1152

LENOX REIGN
USA
www.lenoxreign.com

Lesniewicz Associates
USA
www.designtoinfluence.com

Letterhead Design Studio
Russia
www.letterhead.ru

Lienhart Design
USA
www.lienhartdesign.com

Lightship Visual
Australia
+61894477363

Lindedesign
Germany
www.lindedesign.de

Lippincott
USA
www.lippincott.com

Liquid Agency
USA
www.liquidagency.com

Liquid, inc
USA
303-282-8657

lis design
USA
www.lisdesign.com

Lisa Brussell Design
USA
415-454-7519

Lisa Wood Design
USA
916-961-8744

Liska + Associates Communication Design
USA
www.liska.com

Little Jacket
USA
www.little-jacket.com

The Logo Factory, Inc.
Canada
www.thelogofactory.com

Logo Orange
Romania
+40722143628

logobyte
Turkey
www.logobyte.com

LogoDesignSource.com
USA
www.logodesignsource.com

Logoholik
Serbia
www.logoholik.com

LogoMotto.com
Brunei Darussalam
www.logomotto.com

Looney Design Lab
USA
www.looneydesignlab.com

Loop Design
USA
www.loopdesigngroup.com

LSD
Madrid
www.lsdspace.com

Lukatarina
Slovenia
www.lukatarina.net

Luke Baker
USA
www.creativehotlist.com/lbaker2

lunabrand design group
USA
www.lunabrands.com

Lunar Cow
USA
www.lunarcow.com

Lynde Design
USA
www.lynde.net

Lysergid
France
ww.lysergid.com

M. Brady Clark Design
USA
www.mbradyclark.com

M3 Advertising Design
USA
www.m3ad.com/new

MacLean Design
USA
www.macleandesign.com

MacMillan Lynch
USA
www.mlmedia.ca

Macnab Design
USA
www.macnabdesign.com

Mad Dog Graphx
USA
www.thedogpack.com

mad studios
China
www.mad-studios.com

Madden
USA
863-682-0013

Made On Earth
USA
www.madeonearthstore.com

MAIS VEZES / DZIWANI MONTEIRO
South Africa
www.maisvezes.com

Marc Posch Design, Inc
USA
www.marcposchdesign.com

Maremar Graphic Design
Puerto Rico
www.maremar.com

Mark Oliver, Inc.
USA
805-686-5166

markatos | moore
USA
www.mm-sf.com

Marketing Art + Science
USA
303-337-7907

Marlin
USA
www.marlinco.com

Martin Branding Worldwide
USA
804-282-3100

The Martin Group
USA
www.martingroupmarketing.com

Martin Jordan
Germany
www.martinjordan.de

Mary Hutchison Design, LLC
USA
www.maryhutchisondesign.com

Matt Whitley
USA
479-464-5203

Matthew Wells Design
Canada
www.matthewwells.ca

Mattson Creative
USA
www.mattsoncreative.com

max2o
USA
www.max2oadvertising.com

maximo, inc.
USA
www.maximoinc.com

Maycreate
USA
www.maycreate.com

Mayer Creative
USA
214-924-9037

Mazemedia
USA
www.mazemedia.com

McAndrew Kaps
USA
www.mcandrewkaps.com

McArtor Design
USA
www.mcartordesign.com

mccoycreative
USA
www.mccoycreative.com

McDougall & Duval Advertising
USA
978-388-3100

McGarrah/Jessee
USA
www.mc-j.com

McGuire Design
USA
www.mcguiredesign.com

McQuillen Creative Group
USA
www.mcquillencreative.com

the medium
USA
www.the-medium.net

Meg Levine Design
USA
917-589-8480

MEGA
USA
www.mollyeckler.com

Megan Thompson Design
USA
www.mtdstudio.com

Meir Billet Ltd.
Israel
+5626608

Menikoff Design
USA
206-675-0042

meowork intergrated
Malaysia
www.meowork.com

Methodikal
USA
www.methodikal.net

Metropolis Advertising
USA
www.metropolisadvertising.com

MFDI
USA
570-372-4623

Miaso Design
USA
www.miasodesign.com

Michael Patrick Partners
USA
www.michaelpatrickpartners.com

Mike Quon/Designation
USA
www.mikequondesign.com

Mike Speero
Sweden
www.mikespeero.com

Miles Design
USA
www.milesdesign.com

Miller Creative LLC
USA
www.yaelmiller.com

Miller Meiers Design for Communication
USA
www.millermeiers.com

Minale Tattersfield and Partners Ltd
UK
www.mintat.co.uk

Mindgruve
USA
www.mindgruve.com

MINE™
USA
www.minesf.com

mlQelangelo
Serbia
www.miqelangelo.com

MiresBall
USA
www.miresball.com

Miriello Grafico, Inc.
USA
www.miriellografico.com

Mission Creative
USA
www.missioncreative.biz

Mitre Agency
USA
www.mitreagency.com

Mklane
Italy
www.mklane.com

mod&co
USA
www.modandco.com

The Modern Brand Company
USA
www.themodernbrand.com

Modern Dog Design Co.
USA
www.moderndog.com

Modus Design, Inc.
USA
www.designbymodus.com

Mohouse Design Co.
USA
www.mohousedesign.com

Mojo Solo
USA
651-789-6656

Moker Ontwerp
Netherlands
www.mokerontwerp.nl

Molly&Partners
Italy
+3.9074428195e+011

Monigle Associates Inc.
USA
www.monigle.com

monkeebox, inc.
USA
703-606-9044

Monkey Paw Studio
USA
413-231-2845

Monson Media
USA
www.monsonmedia.com

Monster Design Company
USA
www.monsterdesignco.com

mooci design labs
USA
www.mooci.com

moosylvania
USA
www.moosylvania.com

More Branding+Communication
USA
918-519-1605

Morello+Company
USA
www.morellodesign.com

Morgan/Mohon
USA
www.morganmohon.com

morrow mckenzie design
USA
www.morrowmckenzie.com

Moscato Design
USA
www.moscatodesign.blogspot.com

Moss Creative
USA
www.mosscreative.com

MSI
USA
312-946-6146

mugur mihai
Romania
www.mugurmihai.com

Muku Studios
USA
www.mukustudios.com

Murillo Design, Inc.
USA
www.murillodesign.com

Mystic Design, Inc.
USA
www.mysticdesign.net

Najlon
Croatia
www.najlon.hr

Nanantha Shroff
USA
562-858-4858

Narita Design
Brazil
www.naritadesign.com.br

Natale Design
USA
480-612-5324

Naughtyfish
Australia
+02 93277942

Nectar Graphics
USA
www.nectargraphics.com

neodesign
Taiwan
+886.7.554.8657

NeoGrafica
Costa Rica
506-4400061

NeonBeige
USA
718-928-3903

The Netmen Corp
Argentina
www.thenetmencorp.com

nGen Works
USA
www.ngenworks.com

Nick Glenn Design
USA
www.nickglenndesign.com

Nien Studios
USA
www.nienstudios.com

Nissen Design
USA
503-363-5639

Noble
USA
417-875-5166

noe design
USA
www.noedesign.com

NOMADESIGN, Inc.
Japan
www.nomadesign.jp

Nori Studios
UK
www.noristudios.com

Northfound
USA
www.northfound.com

Nubson Design
USA
701-730-1993

Nynas
USA
214-566-5166

O!
Iceland
www.oid.is

oakley design studios
USA
oakleydesign.com

Object 9
USA
www.object9.com

O'Connor Graphic Design
USA
www.oconnordesign.net

Octane
USA
www.octanestudios.com

Office For Design
South Africa
www.officefordesign.co.za

The Office of Art+Logik
USA
612-599-0286

The Office of Marc Bostian
USA
www.marcbostian.com

Off-Leash Studios
USA
www.offleashstudios.com

O'Hare Design
USA
oharedesign.com

Oluzen
Dominican Republic
www.oluzen.com

Ondine Design
USA
323-316-5843

ONEDRINPEN
UK
www.onedrinpen.com

OPEN
Israel
www.open.co.il

Open Creative Group
USA
www.opencreativegroup.com

Opolis Design, LLC
USA
www.opolisdesign.com

orangebird
USA
614-302-5906

ORFIK DESIGN
Greece
www.orfikdesign.gr

Organi Studios
USA
www.organistudios.com

Origin Studios
USA
www.originstudios.net

orton design
USA
801-691-8244

Oscar Morris
USA
512-293-5954

Oskoui+Oskoui, Inc.
USA
www.oskoui-oskoui.com

Owen Design
USA
www.chadowendesign.com

Oxide Design Co.
USA
www.oxidedesign.com

Page Design
USA
916-457-0108

Pagliuco Design Company
USA
www.pagliuco.com

Pale Horse Design
USA
www.palehorsedesign.com

Pandemonium Creative
Australia
+03 9690 1511

Panic Creative
USA
www.paniccreative.com

Paper Doll Studio
South Africa
+27 11 447 6418

Paper Tower
USA
www.papertower.com

Parachute Design
USA
612-359-4377

Paradox Box
Russia
www.paradoxbox.ru

Paragon Design International
USA
www.paragondesigninternational.
com

Paragon Marketing
Communications
Kuwait
www.paragonmc.com

paralleldesigned
USA
www.paralleldesigned.com

Parallele gestion de marques
Canada
www.parallele.ca

Pat Taylor, Inc.
USA
202-338-0962

Patlejch
Czech Republic
(+420) 602 140 477

Patten ID
USA
www.pattenid.com

Paul Black Design
USA
www.paulblackdesign.com

Paul Svancara
USA
www.svancdesign.com

Pavone
USA
717-234-8886

Peak Seven
USA
www.peakseven.com

pearpod
USA
949-212-7681

Peggy Lauritsen Design Group
USA
www.pldg.com

Pennebaker
USA
www.pennebaker.com

Pense Design
USA
www.pensedesign.com

Pepper Group
USA
847-963-0333

Peterson & Company
USA
www.peterson.com

PETTUS CREATIVE
USA
860-778-5112

Pherra
Romania
www.pherra.com

Philip J Smith
Australia
61415897004

Phinney Bischoff Design House
USA
www.pbdh.com

Phixative
USA
212-534-9058

pictogram studio
USA
301-962-9630

Pierpoint Design + Branding
USA
www.pierpointwebsite.com

Pikant marketing
Croatia
+38548222127

Pink Tank Creative
Australia
www.pinktank.com.au

Pinnacle Design Center
USA
www.pinnacledesigncenter.com

Pix Design, inc.
USA
www.pixdesign.com

Pixel Boy Studio
USA
www.pixelboystudio.com

Pixélion, LLC
USA
www.pixelion.com

Platform Creative Group
USA
206-621-1855

plus1
USA
www.goplus1.com

POLLARDdesign
USA
www.pollarddesign.com

Pomegranate Studio, Inc.
USA
www.pstudio.us

Popgun
USA
www.popgun.com

Porkka & Kuutsa Oy
Finland
www.porkka-kuutsa.fi

PositiveZero Ltd.
UK
www.positivezero.co.uk

PPBH
USA
801-487-4800

Prejean Creative
USA
www.prejeancreative.com

pricedyment
Canada
www.pricedyment.ca

Printt Diseñadores, s.c.
Mexico
(525) 55 5520 6001

Pro Print Designs
Australia
www.proprintdesigns.com.au

Prolific
USA
www.weareprolific.com

Publicis
USA
212-279-7059

Pump Graphic
USA
www.pumpgraphic.com

Pure Brand Communications
USA
www.pure-brand.com

Pure Fusion Media
USA
www.purefusionmedia.com

PureMatter Brand Marketing +
Interactive
USA
408-297-7800

Purple Zante, Inc.
USA
www.purplezante.com

Purplesugar Design
UK
www.purplesugar.com

PUSH Branding and Design
USA
www.pushmybrand.com

Q
Germany
www.q-home.de

Q Design
USA
310-804-1148

Qualitá Design
Brazil
www.qualitadesign.com.br

QueenBee Studio
USA
410-573-1266

Quentin Duncan
South Africa
+27 84 553 1616

R&R Partners
USA
702-228-0222

Rackel Creative
Canada
www.rackelcreative.com

RADAR Agency
USA
www.radaragency.com

Raffaele Primitivo
Italy
www.primitivodesign.com

Rain design partners
Ireland
www.raindesign.com

RAINERI DESIGN
Italy
www.raineridesign.com

rainy day designs
USA
www.rainydaydesigns.org

rajasandhu.com
Canada
www.rajasandhu.com

RAMIKILANI
Jordan
www.ramikilani.com

Randy Mosher Design
USA
www.randymosherdesign.com

Range
USA
www.rangeus.com

RARE Design
USA
www.raredesign.com

Ray Dugas Design
USA
www.cadc.auburn.edu/
graphicdesign/ray.html

Raymond Creative Group
USA
www.raymondcreative.com

Razor Creative
Canada
www.razorcreative.com

RDY
Macedonia
www.myspace.com/rushers-
dieyoung

Reactive Designs
USA
305-790-1885

Reactive Mediums
USA
517-290-6156

reaves design
USA
www.wbreaves.com

Red Circle
USA
612-372-4612

Red Clover Studio
USA
206-683-2314

Red Dog Design Consultants
Ireland
+35314760180

Red Olive Design
USA
www.redolivedesign.com

RedBrand
Russia
www.golovach.ru/works
www.redbrand.ru/projects/field/
catalog3

Redonk Marketing
USA
www.redonkmarketing.com

Redshed Creative Co.
USA
www.redshedcreative.com

Remo Strada Design
USA
www.remostrada.com

renaud garnier smart rebranding
USA
510-653-8809

Respiro Media
Romania
www.relogodesign.com

Retro DC
USA
www.retrodc.com

retropup
USA
973-267-0885

Rhombus, Inc.
USA
www.rhombusdesign.net

Rhumb Designs, Inc.
USA
www.rhumbdesigns.com

Richard Bloom Studio
USA
www.richard-bloom.com

Richard Button Design, LLC
USA
www.buttoninc.com

Richard Harrison Bailey/
The Agency
USA
www.rhb.com

Richard Underberg
USA
www.RichardUnderberg.com

Richard Ward Associates
UK
020 8542 7536

richard zeid design
USA
www.rzdesign.com

Richards & Swensen
USA
801-532-4097

Richards Brock Miller
Mitchell & Associates
USA
www.rbmm.com

Rick Carlson Design
& Illustration
USA
rcarlsondesign.com

Rickabaugh Graphics
USA
www.rickabaughgraphics.com

RIGGS
USA
www.riggspeak.com

Riham AlGhussein
United Arab Emirates
+9.7150443754e+011

Riley Designs
USA
www.rileyhutchens.com

RJ Thompson
USA
www.whatiszola.com

RK Design
USA
847-372-6266

Robert Price
USA
619-792-9668

robin ott design
USA
www.robinottdesign.com

The Robin Shepherd Group
USA
904-359-0981

Robot Agency Studios
USA
www.robotagency.com

Robot Creative
USA
www.robotcreative.com

Rocket Science
USA
www.rocketsciencedesign.net

RocketDog Communications
USA
www.rocketdog.org

Rocketman Creative
USA
www.rocketmancreative.com

Rome & Gold Creative
USA
www.rgcreative.com

Rose/Glenn Group
USA
www.ideasthatmeanbusiness.com

Roskelly Inc.
USA
www.Roskelly.com

Ross Hogin Design
USA
206-443-3930

Ross Levitt
USA
www.createconsume.net

Rotor Design
USA
www.rotordesign.net

Rubber Cheese
UK
www.rubbercheese.com

Rufuturu
Russia
www.zambezy.ru

Rule29
USA
www.rule29.com

Rumfang
Denmark
+4533692070

The Russo Group
USA
www.therussogroup.com

Rusty George Creative
USA
www.rustygeorge.com

RWest
USA
503-223-5443

Ryan Cooper Design
USA
www.visualchili.com

Ryan Graphics
USA
www.ryangraphics.com

Ryder Goodwin
USA
408-472-2264

S Design, Inc.
USA
www.sdesigninc.com

S&N Design
USA
785-539-3931

S4LE.com
Canada
www.s4le.com

Sabet Branding
USA
www.sabet.com

Sabin Design
USA
www.sabindesign.com

Sabingrafik, Inc.
USA
tracy.sabin.com

Sakkal Design
USA
www.sakkal.com

Saltree Pty Ltd
Australia
www.saltreecreative.com

Salty Design Foundry
USA
www.saltydf.com

Same Key Design
USA
www.samekeydesign.com

San Markos
Poland
www.sanmarkos.pl

Sandstrom Partners
USA
www.sandstrompartners.com

Sarah Grimaldi
Italy
www.xister.com

sarah watson design
USA
206-545-8682

Saturn Flyer
USA
www.saturnflyer.com

Sauvage Design
New Zealand
www.sauvage.co.nz

**Savage-Olsen Design
Engineering, Inc.**
USA
251-344-4001

Sayles Graphic Design, Inc.
USA
www.saylesdesign.com

SBE
USA
310-920-8487

Schuster Design Group
USA
972-255-9991

Schwartzrock Graphic Arts
USA
www.schwartzrock.com

scott adams design associates
USA
612-236-1146

Scott Carroll Designs, Inc.
USA
www.scottcarrolldesigns.com

Scott Oeschger
USA
www.scottoeschger.com

Scribblers' Club
Canada
www.scribblersclub.com

Sean Weber
USA
www.flickr.com/seanweber/sets

Sebastiany Branding & Design
Brazil
www.sebastiany.com.br

seesponge
USA
586-255-6514

Selikoff+Co
USA
www.selikoffco.com

Sellier Design, Inc.
USA
770-428-8668

Semisans
USA
www.semisans.com

Shaffer Design Works
USA
www.shafferdesign.com

Sharisse Steber Design
USA
615-945-1099

Shawn Huff
USA
www.shawnhuff.info

Shelley Design+Marketing
USA
www.shelleyllc.com

Shelter Studios
USA
301-942-1901

Sibley Peteet
USA
www.spdallas.com

Sibley Peteet
USA
www.spdaustin.com

Silver Creative Group
USA
www.silvercreativegroup.com

Simon & Goetz Design
Germany
www.simongoetz.de

Simple Creative Design
Canada
www.simplecreative.com

simplegraphics
Russia
www.simplegraphics.ru

Siquis
USA
www.siquis.com

Sire Advertising
USA
www.sireadvertising.com

SK+G Advertising
USA
702-478-4141

Skybend
USA
801-983-6760

Small Dog Design
Australia
www.smalldog.com.au

Smith Design
USA
www.smithdesign.com

Smudge Design Co.
USA
310-980-5005

Sniff Design Studio
USA
www.sniffdesign.com

Sol Consultores
Mexico
www.solconsultores.com.mx

Sommese Design
USA
814-353-1951

Sonia Jones Design
USA
www.soniajonesdesign.com

Soren Severin
Denmark
www.sorenseverin.dk

Sound Mind Media
USA
www.soundmindmedia.net

SoupGraphix, Inc.
USA
www.soupgraphix.com

Spark Studio
Australia
+613 9686 4703

Sparkman + Associates
USA
www.sparkmandesign.com

Special Modern Design
USA
www.specialmodern.com

Spela Draslar
Slovenia
+00 386 31 879 711

Spiral Design Studio
USA
www.spiraldesign.com

Splash:Design
Canada
www.SplashDesign.biz

Spoonbend
USA
www.spoonbend.com

Spork Design, Inc.
USA
www.sporkdesign.com

Squires and Company
USA
www.squirescompany.com

Stacy Bormett Design, LLC
USA
651-748-0872

Steele Design
USA
www.briansteeledesign.com

Sternoskop
UK
www.sternoskop.co.uk

Steve Cantrell
USA
954-574-0601

Steve DeCusatis Design
USA
www.stevedecusatis.com

Steven O'Connor
USA
323-779-5600

Stiles Design
USA
www.brettstilesdesign.com

Stiles+co
USA
www.danstiles.com

Storm Corporate Design Ltd.
New Zealand
www.storm-design.co.nz

Storm Design, Inc.
Canada
www.stormdesigninc.com

Straka-Design
Germany
www.straka-design.net

Strange Ideas
USA
www.baileylauerman.com

Strategy Studio
USA
strategy-studio.com

Stream Creative
USA
414-755-2190

stressdesign
USA
www.stressdesign.com

String
Serbia
+38110322370

Struck
USA
801-531-0122

STUBBORN SIDEBURN
USA
www.stubbornsideburn.com

Studio Cue
USA
www.studiocue.com

Studio grafckih ideja
Croatia
www.sgi.hr

Studio GT&P
Italy
www.tobanelli.it

Studio IX OPUS ADA
The Netherlands
www.floorwesseling.nl

Studio Oscar
UK
www.studiooscar.com

Studio Simon
USA
www.studiosimon.com

Studio Tandem
USA
404-819-4117

Studio3b, Inc.
USA
314-517-1141

Studiofluid
USA
www.studiofluid.com

Stuph Clothing
USA
www.stuphclothing.com

StyleStation
Norway
www.stylestation.net

Subcommunication
Canada
www.subcommunication.com

Sundog
USA
701-476-2384

Sunrise Advertising
USA
www.sunrise-ad.com

SUPERRED
Russia
www.superred.ru

Sussner Design Company
USA
612-339-2886

SVP Partners
USA
203-761-0397

Swanson Russell
USA
www.swansonrussell.com

Switch Branding & Design
South Africa
www.switchdesign.com

switchfoot creative
USA
www.switchfootcreative.com

SwitchStream, LLC
USA
www.switchstream.com

tabula rasa graphic design
USA
www.trgraphicdesign.com

Tactical Magic
USA
www.tacticalmagic.com

Tactix Creative
USA
www.tactixcreative.com

Tandem Design Agency
USA
www.tandemthinking.com

tbg design
USA
tbgdesign.com

Tchopshop Media
USA
504-891-0940

Ten26 Design Group, Inc.
USA
ten26design.com

Tenacious Design
USA
www.tenaciousdesign.com

tesser
USA
415-541-9999

TFI Envision, Inc.
USA
www.tfienvision.com

thackway+mccord
USA
www.thackwayandmccord.com

thehappycorp global
USA
646-613-12220

Thelogoloft.com
USA
www.thelogoloft.com

themarsdesign.net
USA
760-429-3692

Theory Associates
USA
www.theoryassociates.com

Thielen Designs
USA
www.thielendesigns.com

Think Cap Design
USA
713-854-8873

Thinking Cap Design
USA
www.thinkingcapkid.com

Thinking*Room Inc.
Indonesia
www.thinkingroominc.com

Thirtythr33
Germany
www.thirtythr33.de

This Gunn for Hire
USA
619-606-3353

this is nido
UK
www.thisisnido.com

Thomas Cook Designs
USA
www.thomascookdesigns.com

Thorn Creative
USA
www.thorncreative.com

Tim Frame Design
USA
www.timframe.com

Timber Design Company
USA
www.timberdesignco.com

Tip Top Creative
USA
www.tiptopcreative.com

TMCA, Inc.
USA
www.tmcadesign.com

Todd M. LeMieux Design
USA
www.toddlemieux.com

TOKY Branding+Design
USA
www.toky.com

Toledo Area Metroparks
USA
419-407-9735

Tom Martin Design
USA
www.tommartindesign.com

TomJon Design Co.
USA
www.tomjon.net

Tomko Design
USA
www.tomkodesign.com

tomvasquez.com
USA
www.tomvasquez.com

Topo
Spain
www.topo.bz

Torch Creative
USA
www.torchcreative.com

Totem
Ireland
www.totem.ie

Tower of Babel
USA
www.babeldesign.com

Traction
USA
www.teamtraction.com

Traction
USA
www.projecttraction.com

TracyLocke Dallas
USA
www.tracylocke.com

Trapdoor Studio
USA
www.trapdoorstudio.com

Tribe Design LLC
USA
www.tribedesign.com

Tricia Hamon/Pear Tree Design
USA
www.triciahamon.com

Trifecta Design Group
USA
646-912-8387

True Perception
USA
480-330-0720

TrueBlue, Inc.
USA
423-624-0040

TRUF
USA
www.trufcreative.com

Truly Design
Italy
www.truly-design.com

Tunglid Advertising Agency ehf.
Iceland
www.tungl.is

Turner Duckworth
USA
www.turnerduckworth.com

Turnstyle
USA
www.turnstylestudio.com

twentystar
USA
www.twentystar.com

Two Dogs Design
USA
www.twodogsdesign.com

Type Fanatic Design
USA
www.typefanatic.com

Type G
USA
www.launchtypeg.com

Uhlein Design
USA
973-720-3289

UlrichPinciotti Design Group
USA
www.updesigngroup.com

Ulyanov Denis
Russia
www.caspa.ru

Union Design & Photo
USA
www.uniondesignphoto.com

United States of the Art
Germany
www.unitedstatesoftheart.com

UNIT-Y
USA
www.unit-y.com

Univisual
Italy
www.univisual.com

UNO
USA
www.unoonline.com

V V N Design
USA
206-963-2410

Valge Vares
Estonia
+37256215161

Valhalla | Design & Conquer
USA
www.valhallaconquers.com

Van Vechten Creative
USA
619-497-0444

Vanderbyl Design
USA
www.vanderbyldesign.com

VanPaul Design
USA
www.vanpaul.com

Velocity Design Group
USA
www.velocitybrand.com

Vestigio—Consultores de Design, Lda.
Portugal
www.emanuelbarbosa.com

Via Grafik
Germany
www.vgrfk.com

Victor Goloubinov
Russia
www.revision.ru/authors/3187

View Design Company
USA
206-633-4600

Vigor Creative, Inc.
USA
www.vigorcreative.com

Vincent Burkhead Studio
USA
www.vincentburkhead.com

VINNA KARTIKA design
Indonesia
+6281 129 8445

Virgin Mobile USA
USA
908-472-9495

Visible Ink Design
Australia
www.visibleink.com.au

Visual Coolness
USA
www.visualcoolness.com

Visual Inventor Ltd. Co.
USA
www.visualinventor.com

Visual Moxie
USA
www.visualmoxie.com

Visualink Creative
USA
615-771-0500

VIVA Creative Group
USA
www.vivacreativegroup.com

VIVAMEDIA, Inc.
USA
www.virtualviva.com

Vivitiv
USA
www.artomatdesign.com

Viziom
USA
www.viziom.com

vladimir sijerkovic
Russia
www.vladimirsijerkovic.com

volatile-graphics
UK
www.volatile-graphics.co.uk

Voov Ltd.
Hungary
www.voov.hu

Wages Design
USA
www.wagesdesign.com

Walsh Branding
USA
www.walshbranding.com

Webster Design Associates, Inc.
USA
www.websterdesign.com

Welcome Moxie
USA
917-385-2314

Werner Design Werks
USA
www.wdw.com

WestmorelandFlint
USA
www.westmorelandflint.com

Westwerk DSGN
USA
www.westwerkdesign.com

Weylon Smith
USA
www.weylonsmith.com

Whaley Design, Ltd
USA
651-645-3463

WhiteRhino Creative PL
Australia
www.whiterhino.com.au

Whitney Edwards, LLC
USA
www.wedesign.com

William Herod Design
USA
360-297-1288

Willoughby Design Group
USA
www.willoughbydesign.com

Windup Design
USA
www.windup-design.com

WISE Graphic Design
USA
917-378-3880

Wonderfuel
UK
www.wonderfuel.co.uk

WONGDOODY
USA
www.wongdoody.com

Woodend, Nessel & Friends
USA
619-234-2655

Wox
Brazil
wox.com.br

wray ward
USA
www.wrayward.com

www.dannygiang.com
USA
www.dannygiang.com

www.mieland.de
Germany
www.mieland.de

www.yifenglin.com
USA
310-626-7828

www.zka11.com
Bulgaria
www.zka11.com

X RAY
Latvia
www.xray.lv

X-ist
USA
949-202-7716

XY ARTS
Australia
www.xyarts.com.au

Yamamoto Moss Mackenzie
USA
www.ymm.com

yantra design group, inc
USA
www.yantradg.com

yarimizoshintaro
Japan
www.yarimizo.com

Yaroslav Zheleznyakov
Russia
www.y-design.ru

Yellow Dog Design
USA
301-834-6577

Your Eyes Here
USA
www.youreyeshere.com

Zachary Bruno Baltimore Creative
USA
www.zacharybruno.com

ZAYASDESIGN
USA
www.zayasdesign.com

ZEBRA design branding
Russia
+7 8482 537999

Zed+Zed+Eye Creative Communications
USA
www.zedzedeye.com

Zeiber Design
USA
503-756-9641

Zenarts Design Studio
USA
www.tangled-web.com

Zieldesign
USA
www.zieldesign.net

Ziga Aljaz
Slovenia
www.aljaz.org

Zombie Design
USA
www.thedesignzombie.com

ZupiDesign
Brazil
www.zupidesign.com

Zwoelf Sonnen
Germany
www.zwoelfsonnen.de

about the authors

Bill Gardner is president of Gardner Design and has produced work for Cessna, Learjet, Thermos, Pepsi, Pizza Hut, Kroger, Hallmark, Cargill Corporation, and the 2004 Athens Olympics. His work has been featured in *Communication Arts*, *Print*, *Graphis*, the Museum of Modern Art, and New York Art Director publications, as well as many other national and international design exhibitions. He is the founder of LogoLounge.com and the author of *LogoLounge 1, 2, 3, 4,* and *5,* as well as the Master Library Series. He lives in Wichita, Kansas.

Catharine Fishel specializes in working with and writing about designers and their work. A contributing editor to *Print* magazine, she has written for many leading design publications. She is the editor of LogoLounge.com and is author of many books about design, including *LogoLounge 1, 2, 3, 4,* and *5*; *Inside the Business of Graphic Design*; *How to Grow as a Graphic Designer*; *The In-House Design Handbook*; *The Freelance Design Handbook*; and the Master Library Series.